Edu-Chameleon

Leverage 7 Dynamic Learning Zones
to Enhance Young Children's
Concept-Based Understanding

Lili-Ann Kriegler

First published by Ultimate World Publishing 2021
Copyright © 2021 Lili-Ann Kriegler

ISBN

Paperback: 978-1-922497-86-4
Ebook: 978-1-922497-87-1

Lili-Ann Kriegler has asserted her rights under the Copyright, Designs and Patents Act 1988 to be identified as the author of this work. The information in this book is based on the author's experiences and opinions. The publisher specifically disclaims responsibility for any adverse consequences which may result from use of the information contained herein. Permission to use information has been sought by the author. Any breaches will be rectified in further editions of the book.

All rights reserved. No part of this publication may be reproduced, stored in or introduced into a retrieval system, or transmitted in any form, or by any means (electronic, mechanical, photocopying, recording or otherwise) without the prior written permission of the author. Any person who does any unauthorised act in relation to this publication may be liable to criminal prosecution and civil claims for damages. Enquiries should be made through the publisher.

Cover design: Ultimate World Publishing
Layout and typesetting: Ultimate World Publishing
Editor: Marinda Wilkinson

Ultimate World Publishing
Diamond Creek,
Victoria Australia 3089
www.writeabook.com.au

Testimonials

Lili-Ann's presentation skills are excellent – she personalised conversations, used our names, told anecdotal stories and asked for feedback. The pacing of the content was great, with a combination of direct teaching, one on one questions, peer conversations and active engagement which worked well. There was also time for substantive conversation with other participants which helped to solidify our knowledge of the course.

Judith Kahler
Tamborine Mountain State School, Queensland

I thought your presentation was excellent, and the group was wholly engaged and on-task, even when we were tired and a bit brain-fried! You had a lovely mix of stories, anecdotes, physical movement, activities and theory, all presented with your very engaging and gentle style.

Kerry Gambley, Junior Music, SEPC Teacher, EATSIPS Team, QTU
Representative
Tamborine Mountain State School, Queensland

It was a pleasure collaborating with Lili-Ann and her team on the Cognizance Metacognition Project. Her knowledge of the education sector and the passion she showed throughout the project ensured a successful outcome.

Chris Butt
CEO, Cognisess, UK

Lili-Ann and I have worked and travelled together for Independent Schools Victoria for the past eight years. It has been a privilege to do so, and it is rare to meet someone as thoughtful and eloquent as Lili-Ann. She listens, thinks, then expresses ideas fluently, enabling those around her to learn, understand and grow as educators, therapists and parents. Due to her rich experience with children in the early years, the Feuerstein programs, the Reggio Emilia Approach, Bright Start and Systematic Concept Teaching, she possesses a wide base to draw upon. Nothing seems to faze her – she is always a sea of calm and a great team player.

Diane Bourke, Project Manager, Independent Schools Victoria,
Past Junior School Principal Melbourne Girls' Grammar School

I have known Lili-Ann since 2007, when I was a PhD student at the University of Western Australia and she was involved in professional advocacy through the Reggio Emilia Australia Information Exchange. As a head of school, her commitment to bold ideas, professional outreach, and intellectual support of her teachers was evident to me at the time. I have since been privileged to work closely with Lili-Ann in her capacity as consultant for Independent Schools Victoria and I've found her to be a productive, thoughtful, engaged and imaginative collaborator who I could always depend on, and who seminar participants trusted deeply.

Dr Stefania Giamminuti, Senior Lecturer, Early Childhood
Education, School of Education Curtin University, WA

Lili-Ann's knowledge and understanding of education, particularly Early Years, is vast. She has a rich and deep knowledge of the Reggio Emilia principles and practices and has been very closely involved with the dissemination of this approach in Australia including having successfully headed an Early Learning Centre where she implemented this philosophy.

Lili-Ann continues to stretch boundaries and make the connections between theory and practice. She continues to explore the links between emotion and cognition and how this plays out in the classroom. She seeks every opportunity to contribute to current research and further best practice. This, combined with her deep understanding and expertise in teaching, makes her an outstanding educator.

Genia Janover, Past Principal of Bialik College, Melbourne, Ambassador and Principal Advisor at Independent Schools Victoria (ISV)

Lili-Ann Kriegler, in her career as an educator of both children and adults, has made an original and wide-reaching contribution to education in this country. Lili-Ann's personal gifts include a wonderful imagination and extraordinary creativity, combined with a strong curiosity and I have been privileged over many years to witness her work in primary school classrooms as well as early childhood settings, including the design of a wonderful early childhood centre.

Recently in her role at Independent Schools Victoria (ISV), Lili-Ann instigated and maintained the stewardship of an innovative Thinker in Residence project, which culminated in an exhibition displayed in the Atrium at Federation Square, Melbourne. This event illustrates so well the special gifts of Lili-Ann and her ongoing innovative contribution to education in the early years across Australia.

Jan Millikan OAM, Educator, Author and Past President of the Reggio Emilia Australian Information Exchange

Lili-Ann is a wonderful inspiration and mentor who has helped shape our way of thinking in our workplace. Her commitment and vision for meaningful conversations in our work with young children has transformed our practice and supported us to stretch our minds, to look beyond the walls of our practice and design programs that are authentic to the many different ways of thinking and knowing in our young learners – and indeed in ourselves as educators. She is witty, knowledgeable and a pleasure to work with. We look forward to extending our thinking and learning through this new publication.

Debbie Hendren, ELC Director &
Katina Grammatoglou, ELC Educational Leader
Presbyterian Ladies' College, Melbourne, VIC

We have been privileged to work and train with Lili-Ann for several years now. She has a warm and interactive presentation style. She takes theoretical concepts and eloquently presents them in a highly practical and structured way. Lili-Ann has wonderful communication skills: she listens, reflects, ponders and questions in a respectful and thoughtful way.

Lili-Ann has extensive experience and expert knowledge about child development, especially during the early years. She blends this knowledge, theory and practical experience in a very user-friendly way. This book will be an important and practical contribution to the literature for educators who seek to provide evidence-based, creative opportunities for their students.

Mary Williams, Guidance Officer, Prep Teacher and Feuerstein Trainer, &
Jenny Cummings, Prep Co-ordinator and Feuerstein Trainer
Tamborine Mountain State School, QLD

Contents

Introduction 9

Part A: The Eye – Surveying the Landscape 13

   Chapter 1: Be an Edu-Chameleon   15

Part B: The Head – The Construction and Deployment of Concepts 25

   Chapter 2: Two Tiers – Conceptualisation and Cognition   29

   Chapter 3: Vertical Knowledge –
      Power Up Your Curriculum GPS   65

   Chapter 4: Distributed Knowledge   79

   Chapter 5: Concept Transfer – Crossing the Bridge   95

   Chapter 6: Avert the Assessment Avalanche   109

   Chapter 7: In Words We Meet the World –
      Harnessing the Structure of Language   119

Part C: The Body – Calibrate Your Coordinates on the Agility Wheel 135

    Chapter 8: The Agility Wheel — 137

    Chapter 9: Learning Zone 1 – Free Play — 145

    Chapter 10: Learning Zone 2 – Mediated Play — 155

    Chapter 11: Learning Zone 3 – Embedded Concepts — 171

    Chapter 12: Learning Zone 4 – Clarity of Concept — 187

    Chapter 13: Learning Zone 5 – Closed-Ended Mobilisation — 201

    Chapter 14: Learning Zone 6 – Open-Ended Mobilisation — 211

    Chapter 15: Learning Zone 7 – Auto-Generative Creativity — 223

    Chapter 16: The Edu-Chameleon — 237

Part D: The Tail – Edu-Chameleon Lists 253

References 275

Speaker Biography 280

About the Author 281

Acknowledgements 283

Offers 285

Reflections 287

Introduction

Everything is easier if you start with a sense of confidence – and feeling competent is the bedrock of confidence. My wish for this book is that it amplifies your already established competence, and that in turn it bolsters your students' sense of their own competence.

There is little that intrigues and excites me more in my teaching role than seeing children in flow as they challenge themselves to learn, think, create and communicate. Concepts, insights, thoughts, the mastery of techniques and skills – all inspire and interest me whether they are encountered in preschool, primary, secondary or tertiary settings. This is equally true in my consultancy when educators encounter ideas and gain insights that transform their practice.

This book is a synthesis of what I have learned on my journey to understand knowledge at both the atomic level of language and concept acquisition, and at the point where it is mobilised as a profound and marvellous vehicle for problem solving and creativity.

I invite you to do two things. The first is to traverse a structured way of building children's concept formation from a pre-lingual status through to an extraordinarily complex use of language.

The second is to explore seven distinctive learning zones which you can apply at will to facilitate your curriculum design or teaching. Each zone depicts a relational configuration between educators and students. Within each zone, the proximity of the educator to the student changes. In some zones the child has a wide range of choice and freedom. In others, the choices are circumscribed to focus on specific learning goals. The book is a conversation about the agency of both the student and the educator as they purposefully enact their intentions in what I think is the most important endeavour in the world – education.

Throughout my childhood, my parents repeated the mantra: 'no-one can take away your education; it will make you who you want to be'. Who I have become is an educator and I believe that the quality of education is instrumental in creating the quality of society.

I offer you my educational perspective based on what I have learned and experienced over more decades than I care to enumerate here! You will recognise the muses, sages, academics, theorists and philosophies that have influenced me; and I am so grateful to have learned from others and from the long tradition of education that has led us to this moment.

The title *Edu-Chameleon* is a metaphor for the educator's ability to adapt his or her skills, toolkits, knowledge and perspectives, to optimise, understand, plan and assess for different students and for different elements in their context.

The book is designed in four parts which relate to the metaphor of the chameleon:

- Part 1: The Eye – surveys current trends in the early years landscape
- Part 2: The Head – outlines how concepts are formed and deployed in the learning curriculum
- Part 3: The Body – presents seven learning zones, each with its own characteristics
- Part 4: The Tail – is a collection of lists and resources to help you in the classroom.

I wrote this book for leaders, educators and curriculum coordinators in preschool and early primary settings. The ideas have broader application, but I dedicate this book to you and hope that in its pages, you will encounter ideas and information that will inform your practice and add to your knowledge, about knowledge.

PART A

The Eye – Surveying the Landscape

The early years arena is fraught with difficult debates and even divisive issues. In Part A of this book, I present some of these and offer a means of overcoming binary ideas that might cause decision paralysis as educators enact their roles.

CHAPTER 1

Be an Edu-Chameleon

If we know better, we can do better.
Maya Angelou

Would you like to enhance and energise your early years' teaching? The key to positive transformation is trusting your own professional knowledge. Knowledge gives you confidence and clarity when you plan, assess, resource, enact and data track your practice. Your enhanced teaching translates into children's elevated thinking and learning.

This book is for educators of children from three to nine years of age. 'Educator' is an umbrella term for all the early years' professionals working with young children including preschool assistants, teacher-aides, degree qualified teachers, leaders and curriculum coordinators, all of whom enact a vital role. To clarify the terminology, *early years* includes preschool and junior primary education designed for children up to nine years of age.

A key goal for this book, is that it will add value to your practice without adding time to your schedule! The intention is that it will offer you a specifically concept-based lens to review what you already do well.

So, why are you an early childhood educator?

More and more, research indicates that early education is critically important. By the age of five, 90% of the brain's neural networks are laid down (Schonkoff, Phillips & Eds. 2000) and the number of words and quality of language a child has been exposed to, has already started to determine how well he or she will succeed in later life (Suskind 2015).

These are great reasons to be inspired to do the best job you can!

Knowing your practice gives you the ability to develop laser sharp planning and highly efficient assessment and reporting. It gives you assurance in the face of the compliance demands from any education authority your school or centre is accountable to.

Sadly, many early childhood educators, rather than feeling positive, experience a sense of being overwhelmed by expectations – which seem to be coming at them from every direction. More than in any other phase of education, in the early years' arena, there are confusing messages, conflicting philosophies, constant debates and strong opinions. Educators sometimes don't even know if what they are being requested to do is mandatory or just someone's preferred methodology! Teachers end up with decision paralysis, and they don't know where to turn because of conflicting expectations and criticism.

What is the source of the uncertainly and confusion in the early years?

It is commonly believed, and there is ample research to prove it (Singer, Golinkoff & Hirsh-Pasek 2006), that children learn through play. However, the minute we use the word 'play', we polarise the early learning community. Some early primary teachers automatically switch off when they hear it, because their students are not in preschool which they see as the appropriate context for play. In their minds, they have a set learning curriculum, and 'play' does not come into it. Parents have a powerful influence on ideas about play at the primary level, often characterising it is as a waste of time.

Even when the children are in preschool, some parents don't want to hear that their children are 'only playing' at kindergarten.

On the other hand, some early childhood teachers feel as though they cannot directly 'teach' because they are told so often that children learn through play. They develop a hands-off approach and leave the children to it. Yet, as you have just read above, the early years is a critical time for learning.

Children do learn through play, but they don't *only* learn through play.

We must ask ourselves: 'What is at the heart of this debate?' It is something deeper.

The debate is about agency.

Agency is about having autonomy and independence.

There is an opinion, that if preschool teachers engage in direct teaching, they are doing it to the detriment of the young child's independence or creativity. The child ought to be left alone to discover knowledge rather than to have it taught to them directly. There is a common quote that play is a child's work. There is a fear that if content is taught in the kindergarten room the child is being subjected to a push-down curriculum.

Conversely, there is an expectation that young children should become strong, involved learners. If they leave the kindergarten and they are not 'school ready', then the early years teacher has not achieved his or her goals for that child. The result of this paradox is paralysis of action. What do we do?

Many fear that learning too much too early leads to stress and a lack of motivation. There is no doubt this can happen. If students are challenged beyond what the renowned educational psychologist, Lev Vygotsky called their 'zone of proximal development', (Vygotsky 1978); (McLeod 2019) stress could build in the learning relationship, along with frustration, resentment, obstinacy, blocking and many more emotional outcomes. Although we frame learning as a cognitive act, it is in fact, as much emotional as it is cognitive (Feuerstein, Feuerstein & Falik 2009).

At the most simplistic level, emotion might relate to the idea that the child is happy (or not) to accomplish a task. But when we talk about learning emotion, it is more about the energy a child brings to the situation. It is about the motivation to learn. There is a delicate art to maintaining motivation and providing the challenge that is within reach, but not too easy. The zone has a floor and a ceiling – you don't want to move beyond either. So, agency relates to motivation and to autonomy.

In this book we ask:

How can play, thinking and learning cohere in early education to achieve the outcome that both the students and the educators have an equal role; that the agency of both is honoured?

Without motivational energy, without a sense of purpose and autonomy, without a degree of choice, learning loses its lustre.

Further to the above debates, some philosophies want to see young children learning collaboratively in groups, and not as individuals. There is a strong push to develop collaborative projects. The issue then is how to assess and track the progress of the individual child within the group?

In the face of conflicting ideas, educators feel pressured to choose a position. If they accept that children learn through play, they might retreat from planning a structured curriculum and from direct teaching. It is possible that with too much freedom, the child's knowledge won't be elevated during their play. If they want to ensure that students do learn the concepts needed for the child to be school ready, educators might structure the children's content tasks too prescriptively and allow too little freedom. To make sure every child has 'got it' the products are all identical.

If children do not play, they miss out on essential social experience, freedom and volitional activity. If they are not taught, they miss out on the opportunity to develop their knowledge and cognition which forms their immediate knowledge and lays the foundation for their thinking and learning throughout their lives.

None of the elements discussed above arrived out of thin air. There are good reasons for children to play, sound reasons for them to receive tuition, and a long history of structured curricula for children of all ages. There is also great benefit in both individual and collaborative learning.

So, why not use *all of these* learning configurations to our advantage? The debates and divisions don't serve early childhood educators. Rather than saying that direct teaching impinges on a child's freedom, we can reframe this. If we avoid the transmission of knowledge, early years education becomes an island isolated from the education mainland. Rather than thinking of knowledge as forcible transmission, I conceptualise the learning in the early years as a trans-heritance of knowledge. Young children are equally entitled to the knowledge of humanity. Children are thinkers, they are wise, they want to know things. Their learning cannot be disconnected from world knowledge. If we position and distribute it in a way that children richly engage with it, their immersion in it will generate their unique perspectives. They will teach us things that augment our own knowledge. They deserve a serious encounter with knowledge.

An organised, structured introduction to knowledge puts a child in a position to be even more creative, because they have more information and skills to use for creative tasks. We can imagine more complex play, because as knowledge increases, the quality of play spirals to a new and more sophisticated level.

We will benefit from moving away from binary thinking and settle all these positions on a continuum. We can move between them and use the ones that are appropriate for specific goals, or to respond to unique situations in our day. If we don't maximise knowledge and perspectives, each day opportunities for learning, and for quality play, might be irretrievably lost.

In my work as an education consultant and seminar presenter for the past nine years, and before that as a director of early learning, I have realised there is a need to come to grips with the debates. To develop a means for early childhood educators to become confident, agile teachers. We need to become *Edu-Chameleons* so that we can adapt our knowledge and skill to any learning situation.

The work for this book began in conversation with my dear friend and colleague, Helen Schiele, and I acknowledge her part in developing what is now called the 'Agility Wheel'.

What the Agility Wheel allows us to do is to move between different learning zones and bring the requisite skills to any situation.

From my leadership and teaching practice, I've identified seven characteristic learning zones that operate in classrooms. Within each zone, I noticed how the interaction between the educator and the student reorientates. Each zone has specific features and once understood, educators can move between them with purpose. It certainly helped me personally, with planning, assessment, resourcing and reporting. Beyond this, by listening to scores of educators during my consultancy, and reading up on research findings, I gained even greater clarity around these learning configurations. And it is this clarity that I want to share with you in this book.

The seven learning zones are:

- Free play
- Mediated play
- Embedded concepts
- Concept clarity
- Closed-ended mobilisation
- Open-ended mobilisation
- Auto-generative creativity.

Across this continuum, the educator adapts his or her proximity, moving closer when needed; and moving away when not. Each zone has specific goals and interactions, and it is important right from the start to see that these zones are not stages. Rather, they are ways of interacting with children and mediating their learning. The child could be in the middle of free play and the educator might decide to step in for three seconds to directly teach the name of some object or process – and then immediately step away again. Adaptability enables teachers to maximise their artfully arranged learning environment.

The learning zones are presented in detail in Part C, the body of the book.

But before we get there, you will have noticed that several of the learning zones include the word 'concept'. Concepts are how we package knowledge. The next three chapters are devoted to elaborating on the knowledge that underpins these seven learning zones.

From what you have read in this chapter, how would you orient your practice? Are you currently more on the playing or the learning side of the scale? Are your beliefs reflected in the philosophy, vision and curriculum in your school or centre? Did anything surprise you?

Are you ready to continue and find out more about knowledge and the learning zones with each of its specific toolkits?

PART B

The Head – The Construction and Deployment of Concepts

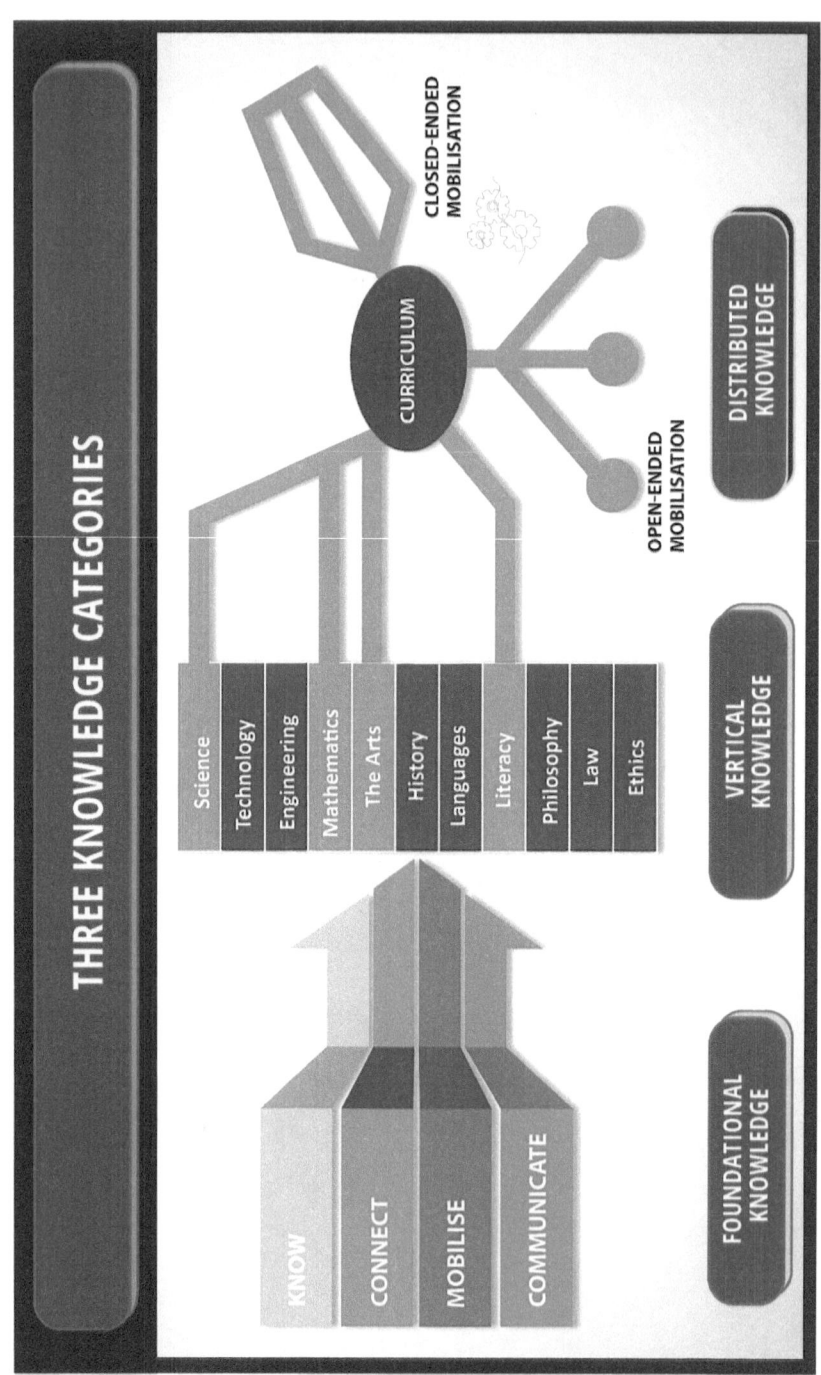

Figure 1: Three knowledge categories

This book is about children's concept-based understanding and how it is supported and scaffolded within the seven distinctive learning zones presented in Part C.

For you to understand how the concepts are constructed and utilised within the zones, I will first familiarise you with how concepts are formed and activated in the learning curriculum.

To do this, I have created a graphic diagram delineating the following three knowledge categories which you will continue to encounter as you read on:

- foundational knowledge
- vertical knowledge
- distributed knowledge.

Foundational knowledge is what all learning is based on, and in the next chapter I will use four terms to explore this: know, connect, mobilise and communicate. Foundational knowledge is represented in the graphic as the basis of all other learning.

Vertical knowledge is a term borrowed from Edward de Bono, who called all existing knowledge 'vertical knowledge'. In the diagram, you will recognise the common table of disciplines on which most curricula are based. Each discipline has its own family of basic concepts and ideas which will be introduced to students as they study it. (De Bono 1998).

Distributed knowledge is a term I created to represent the unique and infinite ways we immerse ourselves in knowledge. Distributed knowledge draws on vertical knowledge, but it is customised, repackaged and redrawn to achieve unique curriculum goals. Distributed knowledge is alive, and is populated by knowledge actors including educators, students, families and communities. It is a creative endeavour that is not bound by what is already known – it is democratic, fully mobilised and dynamic.

The reason for its vibrance is that it is grounded in the present and has a stake in creating the future.

Throughout the book you will find the motifs of closed-ended and open-ended mobilsation. Sometimes we operate in the known, the predictable, the tried and the tested; but often, we research, innovate, project and create. Conceptual understanding is vital for both the closed- and open-ended systems.

In Part B you'll learn the key information needed to understand how concepts are scaffolded and deployed within the seven learning zones.

So let's dive in!

CHAPTER 2

Two Tiers – Conceptualisation and Cognition

Study the science of art. Study the art of science. Develop your senses – especially learn how to see. Realise that everything connects to everything else.
Leonardo da Vinci

Whether you work in the early years, or any other phase of education, your currency is knowledge. Broadly, knowledge is divided into **content** and **process**.

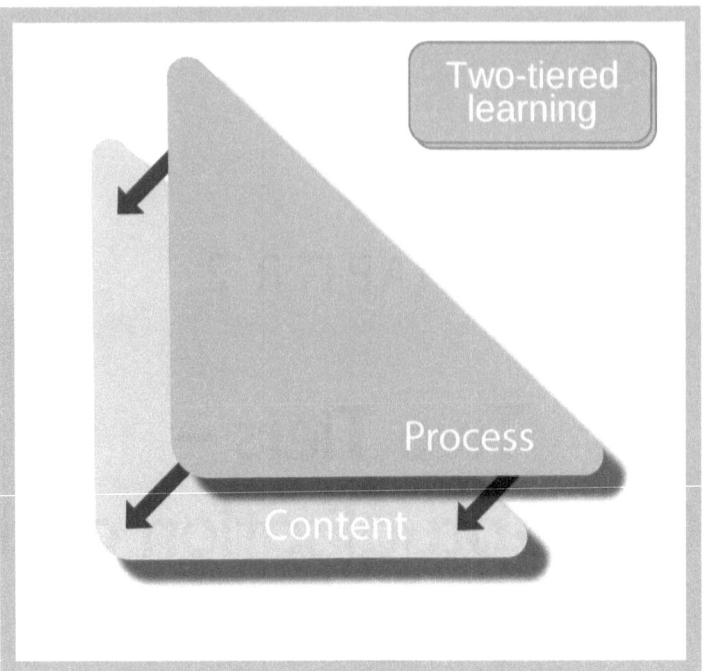

Figure 2: Two-tiered learning

Content is the 'what' and process is the 'how'. Content is conceptual learning – and process is cognition.

What is a concept?

When we look around us, we can see hundreds of things in our immediate environment. A table, a chair, a wall, a flower arrangement, a packet of biscuits, a cat.

Without thinking about it, we use labels to name each of these recognised objects. The label represents an object or idea. By applying a label, we enter conceptual and abstract thinking. When we leave the room, we can 'think' about the cat. We can even think about our specific cat in relation to other cats. We know that cats are pets; and that by virtue of being pets, they are like dogs, goldfish and, in my daughter's case, a six-foot python!

What is process?

In the short discussion above, besides labelling, other processes emerged. Knowing, representing, thinking, comparing, categorising, recollecting, connecting, remembering. These are all processes for managing knowledge.

When we are alerted to our thinking process, and consciously deploy it, we are thinking at another level. Understanding our thinking is metacognition. I recently attended an online course with a British early childhood specialist, Dr Ruth Deutsch, to learn about the 'Bright Start' program developed by Carl Haywood. She said, *'You can't start to develop metacognition too early!'* And there is research to back the benefit of explicitly teaching metacognition (Ellis, Denton & Bond 2013); (Ronilo 2018). When I say explicitly teaching, I don't mean teaching the skills in isolation. I believe in including reference to them in context while teachers and students are approaching, acquiring and consolidating content.

Two types of concepts

Concepts are separated into two types: lower order, and higher order.

Lower order concepts are labels for the objects, features and ideas as single specific instances in the real world. For example, I have a short ruler on my desk.

Higher order concepts are more generalised and refer to a *group* of lower order concepts that share key features/criteria and make them eligible to be included in a category. A 'ruler' is part of a category called 'instruments of measurement' and shares the category with a thermometer, a barometer, a metronome and a bathroom scale. Besides cataloguing objects into categories, we can catalogue the features of an object. 'Short' belongs to the category 'size' and is similar to words like: big, small, medium, miniscule, expansive and tiny.

Higher order concepts are efficient because they are transferable across contexts. If I know about 'size' as a concept, I can use it in maths, geography, literacy, dressmaking, carpentry, surgery and many other contexts. Packaging information in high order concepts is one of the ways we can teach for transfer.

Categories help us organise content. Specific experiences relate to general knowledge. It is easier to learn new concepts if they can be packaged together under an umbrella concept. The superordinate umbrella category is high order thinking. The examples under the umbrella are subordinate lower order concepts.

Content knowledge, from the simplest to the most complex is conceptual. Process knowledge, how we manage, use, organise and deploy concepts is cognition.

Once, when I was discussing how we think with four-year-olds, a child, Daniel, described how in his brain he had a huge cupboard with hundreds of tiny drawers. He put an idea in a drawer and remembered where it was. When he wanted it again, he just opened the drawer and took it out. His metaphor is quite useful. What is in the drawers is the content. The cupboard and the drawers are the structure for how the content is organised and the action of knowing where the drawers are, opening them, retrieving the knowledge and using it, is the process.

There are two things to say about this metaphor. First, we don't want the structure for our knowledge to be set in stone. So, systems thinking is a better metaphor from our perspective. If one thing changes in a system, everything adjusts. In systems thinking, we don't end up with old information in the drawers that is no longer relevant, true or appropriate. The system updates to reflect new information. Jean Piaget's terms 'assimilation' and 'accommodation' are good for explaining this. Assimilation is how you understand it at first and accommodation is how it changes in the light of new information (Piaget & Cook 1952).

The second thing to say about conceptual information and cognition is that the distinction can become confusing, and for good reason.

If I talk about comparison, I am labelling a mental activity. Therefore, it is a concept. But if I am engaged in the act of comparing, if I am in the flow of it, then it is a process. Cognition is the act of using the thinking process.

I can put 'comparison' in one of Daniel's drawers. I can even put a variety of systems for comparison in the drawer. While I am comparing all the drawers and selecting which drawer to put them into, I am mobilising cognition. Cognition happens in the present. It is a current state. If I say now that yesterday I was comparing things, it is a memory and it's a piece of content. As I am writing this, I am processing. I am trying to organise the concepts in a particular order so that they are comprehensible to you. When I read this back, it is already content.

There are labels and definitions for thinking processes (content) and there is the active minute by minute use of the processes (cognition).

Knowing your knowledge

Several years ago, I designed an educational leadership seminar series attended by preschool and lower primary leaders, curriculum coordinators and educators. Over several encounters, they were challenged to define their educational philosophy and curriculum vision. Despite knowledge being central to their work, uncertainty about knowledge came up as their number one concern! It was a surprise to all of us. And it wasn't merely a lack of clarity about planning an appropriate curriculum. There were questions about assessment, reporting, compliance, communication with parents and forging relationships with specialists. What we realised was, that they couldn't fully distinguish between the different kinds of knowledge they were offering. They hadn't consciously and purposefully defined, evaluated or curated it in their minds, so it was not being done on paper.

The first distinction was the one we discussed above, that learning is either conceptual or cognitive. But there are more refined ways of looking at knowledge. After grappling with knowledge for years, as indicated above, I conceptualised it as foundational, vertical and distributed.

After expanding on these knowledge types, the participants were on firmer ground in matching their curriculum planning to reflect their educational ideals. They were also clearer about how to arrange and resource their play and learning environments. With a high-level vision in place, and more certainty about content and thinking, they worked out ways to evaluate students' learning that dovetailed with their values and vison. They became much more confident about enacting their leadership roles.

A valuable insight gained during this seminar series was that what you see, is often limited by what you're looking for. If you know more, or expect more, you find more. Their planning and especially their evaluation became more targeted to match their goals.

Acquiring and consolidating concepts is easy for some children, occurring as if by osmosis. But mostly there is no consistent, automatic maturational path. It helps considerably if children are alerted to concepts, become conscious of them and consolidate them within the immediate contexts where they occur (Kinard & Kozulin 2008).

Let's focus on foundational knowledge. Over time, I have abbreviated it in my mind to four words: know, connect, mobilise, communicate.

Four components of foundational knowledge

An in-depth understanding of the four components (know, connect, mobilise and communicate) will set you and your students up for success.

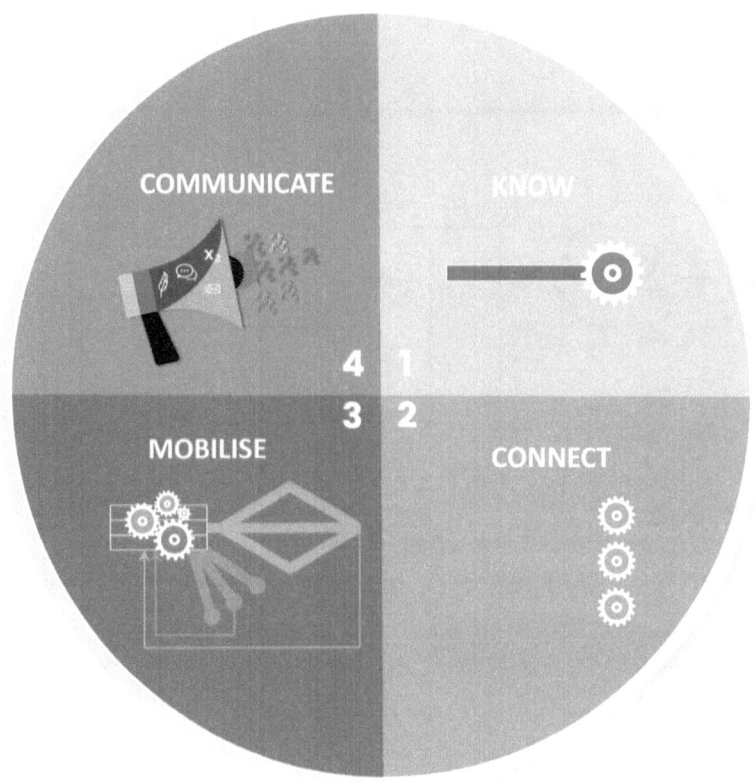

Figure 3: Graphic representation of four components of foundational knowledge

I would like to explore each of these foundational knowledge entry points with you in detail, so that, you (like the educators referred to above) have the opportunity to distinguish, evaluate and curate them. You might decide how they align with your own vision, or the philosophical ideals of your content. You can determine if and how they operate in your day-to-day work, and perhaps be inspired to incorporate them more consciously into your own planning and evaluation. As we go along, you will see that the thinking processes are discussed alongside the content, and key process words are listed for each of the four components for reference.

Take a deep breath!

Figure 4: Pictorial representation of four kinds of knowledge

KNOW

Perception

Before we can use knowledge in any way, we need to be aware of it. From birth, children are constantly learning to recognise things and assign meaning to them. There is an order.

First the child receives information through all their sensory pathways. Next through repeated exposure, they recognise a pattern. The pattern can be a series of events, which become predictable, or the recognition of an entity. (Of course, they don't use the word 'entity'! They just know that it tastes good and it comes regularly – like milk!) An infant hears footsteps, next they are raised up and finally they are hugged warmly. Parent, grandparent, some lovely entity. They recognise the bottle and know it contains the drink they like and need. Over time, they give meaning to the sensory experiences, patterns and entities. Much later they learn to name and label them. Sensing, without assigning meaning, is just sensing. Assigning meaning to an experience is perception. So, the first step in *knowing* something, is perception (Yasnitsky et al. 2014).

Children know things before they can label them. They build up experiential schemas (a bit like a sensory memory) in their mind that they may not have a word for (Hill 2016); (Atherton & Nutbrown 2013). This kind of knowledge, phenomenology, is gathering information from immediate experience from a personal point of view. Sensory experiences become motor-perceptual memories. And that is exactly what young children are gathering when they play, which illustrates why play is so important.

Later in life, say, in a science laboratory, the knowledge of how liquid moves in a bucket, learnt as a child, enables a researcher not to spill sulphuric acid from a beaker onto a bench. Students amass multitudinous sensory memories in their minds as they learn how the world works.

Figure 5: Fairy incursion - fixing broken wing

An example of sensory understanding occurred during a storytelling drama incursion organised when I was still teaching. The performer, Hannah Greenwood, was dressed as a fairy called 'Little Sky Blue'. During the performance, her wing was damaged by a storm and the children were invited to 'fix it' for her.

Clearly, she was not fairy-sized! After her performance we asked the children if she was 'real'? We were not surprised that they said, emphatically, 'NO!' What *was* surprising was that it had nothing to do with her size, which they could easily have articulated. It was the quality of her wings.

They couldn't tell us that real fairies' wings are diaphanous, insubstantial, fragile or ethereal … because they didn't have the vocabulary. But they did have the concept. And they tried to tell us by using their hands, demonstrating these ideas with soft fluttery movements and gestures.

Learning is not straight off facts. It is a fact when you have a name for it and you can share and articulate it, but you can know about it long before that. This is important to keep in mind in the early years, because 'qualities' or 'feelings' of things, is what children are internalising when they play with and manipulate a vast array of materials every day. A child learns about balancing water in a bucket by experiencing balancing water in a bucket many times. Sometimes many times in one day!

Attaching labels

Beyond experiential schemas, where children know things without naming them, we move on to where they do learn labels for them. There may be a stage where they give their own partial words or names for things. Grandpa is 'da'. These will be understood by people in their circle. It is idiosyncratic language. Some identical twins develop an entire idiosyncratic language only they understand!

It makes me think of the wonderful scene in the Disney version of *The Little Mermaid* where the seagull, Scuttle, knowledgeably informs the mermaid, Ariel, that a fork is a *dinglehopper*: 'Humans use these little babies to straighten their hair out! Just a little twirl here, and I have an aesthetically pleasing configuration of hair that humans go nuts over!' How was Ariel to know any different?

Having the facts, knowing what something is, is important knowledge. But it is static. Very often, in early years, and indeed, other educational settings, all an educator is asking for is recognition.

'What shape is this?'

'A square.'

'Great answer.'

This 'great answer' is only the beginning! We will discuss this in more detail later.

Visualisation

A stage beyond recognising an entity and naming it, is the ability to hold a mental image of it in your mind. This visualisation or mental imagery is vital because it enables us to think about things that are not immediately perceptible. A child recognises that there is a chair in front of them *in situ*, but they also need to picture it when it is not there! Some people, believe it or not, do not have this ability. It's called *aphantasia*. When I first heard this, I was agog, because holding pictures in my mind is second nature to me. Right now, I see, and smell, a virtual coffee!

Mental images are the immediate way we begin to represent the real world in our mind. It moves us from the concrete here and now into the abstract world. Children learn to name and picture things in their minds.

But we want children to do more than know what something is. We want them to connect their knowledge to everything else. I love the way da Vinci puts this idea in the quote at the start of this chapter. Quite simply, 'everything connects to everything else'.

Thinking is habitual. We get used to doing it in a particular way. If we want children to spontaneously try to connect the dots between different pieces of information, to put it in a broader context, we must encourage them to do it regularly so they lay down a neural pathway to do it. We want connecting to become habitual. We want them to have a neural superhighway for connecting stuff.

> *Process words: sensing, experiencing, focusing, perceiving, recognising, assigning meaning, remembering, labelling.*

IN SUMMARY:

- infants commence knowing things from birth (and possibly before)
- information enters through the sensory pathways
- the brain responds to, and begins to interpret, patterns in entities and events
- when the pattern or sensation is assigned meaning, it is perception
- children may have experiential schemas in their mind before they can name and label what they know
- in a social or educational setting, the pieces of knowledge are given names and labels
- initially the labels may be idiosyncratic, and understood only by people close to the child
- finally, conventional names and labels are ascribed to both concrete and abstract entities
- the same or similar entities are recognised in diverse contexts
- the entity is available as a mental image which represents the real thing in the real world.

CONNECT

There are many ways to connect knowledge. Perhaps the most logical place to start is to connect something to itself – internal connections.

Whole and parts

Beyond recognition, knowledge becomes more complex; and we don't have to go too far to explore this complexity. We can start by simply unpacking the whole and parts of a single entity. (I know! I love the word entity! 'Object' just does not do it for me. I can't think of a tree or a dog as an object.)

An entity is something with an individual and specific existence. It has boundaries. In this case, let's use the square mentioned earlier. If we extend thinking past recognition, we can unpack the features of a square. Four equal straight sides, four 90° corners. (And there are MANY more features of a square.) If our entity is a mandarin – then the features are that is has an inside and an outside. The outside is peel, the inside is segments. It has juice in it.

As you can see, the minute we start to unpack the whole and parts of a single thing, we are already connecting. We identify relationships between the whole and the parts. The mandarin segments are a curved shape and they are triangular at the top. This is so that they nest together in the cylindrical shape of the fruit. If we go from the whole and unpack the parts we are analysing. If we go from the parts, see how they work together, and pack them back, we are synthesising. Synthesis and analysis are also sometimes called inductive and deductive reasoning.

Just to challenge everything I just said, a whole is not always one integral thing. For example, a team, consisting of eleven players is a whole.

Comparison

From doing a whole and parts analysis of an individual entity, we move on to comparing one thing to other things. It makes sense, at first, to compare what is the same or similar about the things we are focusing on. Then later to explore what is different.

Initially the square may be compared to a rectangle, the mandarin to a lemon. They have several similarities.

When we connect ideas, we understand the features of each individual thing; then we focus on the similarities and differences in those features in something else. With regards to the rectangle and the square, they are similar in all except one feature. The square has four sides the same length. The rectangle has two sets of two equal sides. If you think about it, a square is actually a special occurrence of a rectangle ... but we're veering off track!

The mandarin, first compared to a lemon, is later compared to a banana, which despite being a fruit, is very different according to several features: shape, structure, flavour, texture, etc.

Comparison is not so much a single thinking skill as it is a compact battery of individual skills. In general, we have a focus entity A and a target entity B. We observe the focus and target entities in detail, have a goal for the comparison, determine the criteria for comparison, discard what is irrelevant, and come to a conclusion about the comparison process (Feuerstein et al. 1980).

Comparison makes thinking more efficient

So, what can comparison relate to? Comparison denotes how things are equivalent, similar or different, by size, distance, volume, height, form, position, weight, orientation, function, age, effort, complexity, beauty, value, temperature ... capacity to annoy you?

Each of these criteria gives us a specific kind of information. There are endless ways of connecting information through comparison and it gives us clarity about one thing in the light of another thing.

When comparing two of their friends, children select specific criteria rather than doing a hazy comparison. They compare height, hair colour, loyalty, personality and many other features. We call this ability comparing apples with apples. This kind of targeted thinking and comparing is a very transferable skill.

A further fundamental aspect of comparison is to keep track of what remains the same and what has changed or transformed. For example, if six oranges have been cut in quarters, there are 24 pieces, but the fact remains that all the parts originate from six oranges. This is the conservation of constancy – tracking what is the same.

When we match things that are similar, we begin to sort them into groups.

Categorisation/classification

When things are similar, like the mandarin and the lemon, we can categorise them. In this case they belong to the superordinate category: citrus fruits. A superordinate category is the next group up from the element we are dealing with. Mandarin is a citrus fruit, next up is fruit, next up might be food type.

The square and the rectangle belong to the superordinate category: two-dimensional linear shapes because they are composed of straight lines and they enclose an area. Categorisation and classification do the job of being umbrella words for elements that belong together. Dedre Gentner, a foremost language researcher, has demonstrated that comparison processes are central in children's learning of relational knowledge in categories (Gentner 2005).

You will no doubt see how this brings order and organisation to our knowledge. It has been doing so since time immemorial. For instance, in the discipline of biology, animals and plants have long been classified into different species.

It is important to remember that depending on the feature that is the focus, *a single entity can belong to more than one category*. A red circle can belong to a colour category and shape category. This is the basis of Venn diagrams. A person may be a sibling and a spouse.

Categorisation has two parts: the superordinate category and the elements. Let us say that a child is out in the rain. Someone says, 'It's wet weather today,' which gives us some information.

We could just park that.

But, what if the person says, 'Do you remember the other day when it hailed? That was really stormy weather! What do you think hail is made of?'.

The child might respond: 'It was made of ice and I know ice is made of water! It made my hands freezing!'

The companion asks: 'And what is rain made of?'

'Water.'

'Yep, and is there any other weather where water is important?'

The child is building up a repertoire of knowledge about weather. The superordinate concept starts to inform the elements, and the elements make the superordinate category clearer too. This is a two-way mechanism for consolidating meaning and information. When they encounter snow, sleet, drizzle, mizzle, mist or fog, they might have a better understanding about weather; and each of these unique kinds of weather. Categories are a way of generalising knowledge. Going from the specific and particular to the universal. The universal is good for transfer.

In his future-focused education, Lee Watanabe-Crockett describes a series of questions called herding questions which move progressively from the specific to the general. At the general level, everyone can think about an issue from exactly where they are (Watanabe-Crockett 2018). If we apply this idea in the early years, we might get something like this:

- Is Robin a good friend?
- Is Robin a better friend than Jules?
- What is a good friend?
- What is friendship?

Or:

- Do you like the rain?
- Is rain better than wind?
- Which is your favourite kind of weather?
- What is weather?

So, effort spent connecting the specific to the general is time well spent.

Identifying connection in children's speech

Here is an example of the ideas of four-year-old friends, Harry and Nicholas, who are considering the weather:

Harry: 'This time is when the weather changes. It changes to different times for the year.'

It is clear that Harry relates weather to another concept: time. This conversation could be extended if we ask him what happens at different times of the year. We could ask him to elaborate his knowledge.

When Nicholas, is asked to comment he says:

'We're at the first sign of what he said. It's not the cold season yet, because the cold season is after the hot season and it's next term or next year. It can change. It's like rain, or a storm or the deep snow … but I haven't seen that here. But I saw it on the TV when Mole was inside and the snow was on the outside and sometimes it's dark and sometimes it's light …'

Nicholas's response is almost like James Joyce's novel *Ulysses*, famous for its stream of consciousness! He moves through multiple concepts and contexts within this short capture.

First, he acknowledges that he is responding to Harry's earlier contribution. He recognises the convention of picking up a thread and responding within a recognised discourse. Then, we follow Nicholas as he thinks about the sequence of time in seasons, school terms and, the light or dark of passing days. He distinguishes between kinds of weather. Indicates that he has not experienced extreme weather in this place in the same way as he did in another place he remembers. We hear about his pastime of watching television in relation to his literary knowledge of Kenneth Grahame's character, Mole, from *Wind in the Willows*. He also throws in some references to orientation in space, referring to 'here' meaning Australia, as opposed to England, his country of origin. And he uses the spatial terms: 'inside' and 'outside'. The interweaving of ideas is like a complex and beautiful thought-melody.

We could continue the conversation with Nicholas to solidify or extend his understanding of the concepts he is tapping into in his conversation, but already, he is great at connecting ideas.

Knowing and connecting as static knowledge

So far in this discussion we see the connection of information, but we are still in an area of static knowledge. We have information about single entities and how they are the same or different from others. We can see the relationships between them. The knowledge is not yet mobilised.

But don't underestimate the immense value of this knowledge. If we don't know exactly what criteria, attributes or features things have, and how they are the same or different from one another, the concepts won't be consolidated enough to mobilise them!

A rider to interject here is that some readers might be thinking, 'Surely this kind of matching and understanding relationships is mobilising knowledge?' If the thinking is used in evaluation and decision-making, it is mobilisation. If it is just noting the relationships, it is static.

There is a black car and a red car. You know the horsepower of each. Static knowledge.

You want to decide which to buy. The black car has more horsepower and will give more grunt. You mostly drive your car in an urban area with speed limits from 50–100 kmph. You are concerned about safety, and red is more visible. Your favourite colour for cars is black. Based on these considerations, which car would you choose? Mobilised knowledge.

A second way comparison is mobilised is in figurative language. In literature, or in life, things are often compared in an abstract way, which dislocates its meaning from its original location. 'His skin was yellowed parchment.' In this metaphorical language, parchment, old-fashioned writing material, is used to describe someone's skin. This employs inferential thinking. You are not told directly but have to infer what it means by transferring features of parchment to describe skin.

Process words: focusing, attending, analysing, synthesising, comparing, relating, categorising, evaluating, decision-making, inferring.

IN SUMMARY:

- when we connect an object to itself, understanding is gained of the internal relationships between a whole and the features of its parts
- we compare using a compact battery of subskills
- we compare a focus entity A to a target entity B
- we select specific features or criteria to compare by
- we discard irrelevant information
- we come to a conclusion about the equivalence, similarity or difference of a specific feature between focus A and target B
- it is generally more efficient, when teaching, to commence comparison by observing what is the same or similar: and then progressing to what is different
- when we understand the criteria, similarities, and differences, we are in a position to categorise or classify information
- categorisation promotes deeper understanding about both the umbrella concept and the elements within it
- connection helps to locate and organise knowledge for easier learning, retrieval, mobilisation and transfer.

MOBILISE

As we have seen, connected knowledge, even if it is static, is extremely important. But knowing and connecting knowledge are different from mobilising knowledge.

When we mobilise knowledge, we apply it to achieve a goal. For example, making a decision is mobilising knowledge, because we are evaluating something and projecting the consequences of a course of action.

How do children mobilise knowledge?

A young child usually knows the colours, blue, red and yellow. He or she connects that shades of blue are similar in colour to the primary colour blue; that blue is different from yellow; and that all three are colours. The child mobilises the knowledge when something is done with it.

Children might sort the colours into groups. For instance, this often happens when children are playing with blocks and other loose parts. They use all the blue wishing stones in one area, all the green in another and all the yellow somewhere else. They might have the blue stones represent water, and the green ones, grass.

Once they learn that you can create secondary colours by mixing the primary colours, they activate the knowledge at the painting easel as they try to get the exact colour orange to paint marigolds. They might even add white to lighten their colours.

At the primary level, students know the addition and subtraction symbols in maths, and apply their knowledge when they use the symbols to solve equations.

They understand what a magnet is, and they use one to move a puppet they have designed across a board with the magnet underneath and out of view.

Mobilisation is the active use of knowledge

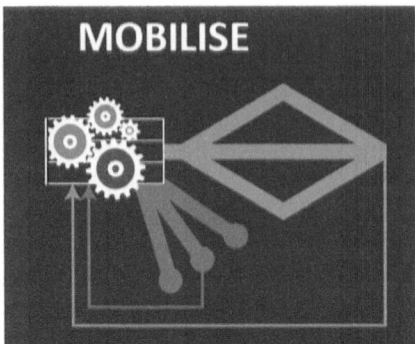

Figure 6: Closed-ended and open-ended mobilisation

I will unpack this further to explain the two main kinds. The first kind, closed-ended mobilisation, has a predictable outcome, while the second is open-ended. For knowledge to be mobilised, several elements need to be activated and work together to achieve a goal.

Predictable or closed-ended mobilisation

Predictable mobilisation is when we use information towards a known goal. This is usually when specific information needs to be mastered and used during application tasks. Once a child has learned a new idea or unit of work, you might provide exercises, or arrange materials to achieve a task. Children learn about balance, and they learn how to make things balance. Solving maths problems, using heat to melt ice, using a plan to write an essay. In all these scenarios, knowledge is mobilised, but we know what we are trying to achieve. If we are doing a jigsaw puzzle, or solving a crossword, we need to activate several kinds of knowledge, but we know where we are going with it.

Problem-solving with a predictable outcome is not necessarily easy. It can be anything from simple to extraordinarily complex.

Like comparison, problem-solving is also a compact battery of sub-skills. First and foremost, we have to define the problem, then we harness or develop a procedure for solving it. We gather all the pieces of information; we plan and then we manipulate the parts or steps to achieve the end result. We need to prioritise the steps into a sequential order. We go through the procedure and reach a solution or conclusion.

This is more than connecting knowledge, it is using it as a vehicle to get to a new product or destination.

In some tasks, the sequence of the steps is more important than in others. You can't put a cake into an oven until the batter is mixed. But you might assemble a model aeroplane in several non-sequential steps towards the concluding step. Sometimes the steps are reversible; I can undo a jigsaw puzzle but I can't un-bake a cake. (Actually, I struggle to even bake a cake!)

An example here might help as we move from predictable to open-ended mobilisation. As a primary school teacher, you will have been teaching addition, subtraction and possibly the beginnings of multiplication and division.

Predictable mobilisation has you develop 12 problems for your students using the operations that have just been covered.

Next, to ramp up the challenge, and use an open-ended mobilisation, you set a challenge to find 17 ways that 17 is the answer. This problem is so widely opened, that you wouldn't possibly be able to predict everything your students come up with. Some might stick to addition and just add up different numbers. Others might use a combination of all the operations. If you are lucky, some of them will bring in knowledge that you haven't taught yet, and surprise everyone. Open-ended mobilisation is the bridge to creativity.

Open-ended mobilisation

There are many times in life where we act with no precise or known outcome, harnessing our current state of knowledge and using our best assessment to project or imagine what might eventuate. This kind of mobilisation can go in more than one direction, with different possible outcomes. But we still need a process to activate our intention.

Like problem-solving, in open-ended mobilisation, we will have some goal in mind. Usually, we visualise or imagine what we are trying to solve or achieve. Even if we are just feeling our way, like selecting a fabric, we monitor what we are feeling to make a decision. We use our experience to formulate a process. We use thinking skills like hypothesising, imagining, modelling, evaluating and creating. Hypothesising is if…then thinking. As an educator, you would like children to hypothesise. When they don't know the exact answer – it is something to be verified or discovered. Most scientific investigation is based on hypothetical thinking.

It is not an accident that this kind of thinking is seen as high order thinking and is usually at the top of any knowledge taxonomy. This includes the well-known and enduring Benjamin Bloom's taxonomy (Guskey 2001), the revised Bloom's taxonomy (Eds. Anderson et al. 2001) and the work of John Biggs and Kevin Collis on Solo Taxonomy (Biggs 2016). In Biggs and Collis' work, this high order inventiveness is called the *extended abstract*. When I read it, I always imagine a figure at the edge of earth's sphere, holding out a butterfly net, trying to catch the stars. To bring this image to life, I had an amazing artist, Iulian Thomas in Romania, on a platform called Fiverr, draw it for me, and for you!

The Nobel nominee, and cognitive psychologist, Reuven Feuerstein also created a comprehensive taxonomy of 28 cognitive functions categorised under input, elaboration and output (Feuerstein et al. 1980).

We know automatically, I think, that primary school children will use high order mobilised thinking. But you might ask, 'Do preschool children do this?'

Figure 7: Child pursuing knowledge – extended abstract

I spoke about the fairy incursion above. The incursion was based on a playground conversation I had with a child during outdoor play, which later developed into a research project with the group.

I was sitting on a bench and a child came and stood directly in front of me, eye to eye. (This is an object lesson in itself. I don't think she would have done it if I was standing at that time.) She said, 'Mrs Wriggler (translation: Kriegler, and, yes, we did use the formal surnames!), I was thinking about making some wings. I was imagining my sewing machine … and my wings will have some web patterns on them'. Then she was quiet for a minute, looking at my upper body and shoulders, and continued: 'I can't lend you them.' Quiet contemplation …, 'But, I can make you some. I will need a *much* bigger sewing machine'. Then she turned and skipped off on her tiptoes, fluttering her arms and humming to herself.

Astounding. Not only had she combined and mobilised several sources of information about how to make wings, but she had calibrated what she would have to do to adjust her project to accommodate my dimensions! She had mentally compared size, shape and functionality of sewing machines, to compare focus A and target B entities; she and me. She had perceived a problem, used all the pieces of information at her disposal, applied logical reasoning and hypothesised that a bigger sewing machine was just the ticket!

Later that day my co-teacher and I asked her to explain her ideas to her peers in a group meeting. We asked whether she would like to try and make some wings the following day. She thought that was a grand idea. Other children got excited – and it launched a project about wings of so many different kinds. Birds, butterflies, fairies, dragons; and the mechanical wings for planes and rockets. Her wings stretched into zoology, fantasy, engineering and science.

Mobilised, high order thinking is definitely at home in the kindergarten.

Figure 8: Dragon wings – Joshua, 4 years old

Linking back to agency

After the discussion in these first three sections of the chapter, a predictable conclusion might be that you see the mobilisation of knowledge as much more important than static knowledge. In the last decade or so, there has been much written and discussed about content knowledge not being that important, and that the emphasis should be on the process. You will also hear people say that the process is more important than the product. I am a great believer in process. But I'm also a great believer in content and in product.

At the 12th International Conference of Thinking (ICOT) in Melbourne in 2005 (Curriculum & Leadership Journal Website 2005), I was excited to attend an address by the global expert on creativity, Edward de Bono. He raised the point about how educators value content versus process. He said that content was highly necessary in creativity. When you are creating, you consciously – or in a wonderful unconscious aha moment

– put together two disparate elements in a new relationship. A new idea, solution, humorous comment, or illumination occurs. He gave to indicate that the more children know, the more likely they are to be able to generate creative ideas. De Bono calls traditional knowledge 'vertical knowledge', which he sees as 'effective but incomplete' and which needs to be supplemented with the 'generative qualities of creative thinking'. He states, 'there is no antagonism between the two sorts of thinking. Both are necessary. Vertical thinking is immensely useful but one needs to enhance its usefulness by adding creativity and tempering its rigidity' (De Bono 1998).

From De Bono's statements and the discussion above, we can see that there is a close relationship between static and mobilised knowledge: they fuel each other. When we know and use information, we gain experience and skills. We reach a new platform. From that new launching point we can take on a more complex challenge. *But we can't go from zero to full throttle without fuel.* When we say that we need to offer children open-ended activities in order not to impinge on their creativity, we should also say, don't put them in that situation without the knowledge or process required for them to embrace and enjoy the challenge. Sir Ken Robinson considered the two in this way: 'Imagination allows us to think of things that aren't real or around us at any given time, creativity allows us to do something meaningful with our imaginations' (Robinson & Aronica 2010).

In honour of the now late, Sir Ken's comments, how do you use your imagination and creativity?

> *Process words: applying, decision-making, organising, planning, problem-solving, logical reasoning, sequencing, prioritising, concluding, imagining, hypothesising, creating.*

IN SUMMARY:

- mobilised learning begins when we apply static knowledge in an organised way to reach a goal
- mobilised learning can be either predictable or open-ended
- predictable mobilisation can be generally seen as problem-solving
- open-ended mobilisation is also goal-oriented, but the outcome is not generally known and could have several pathways
- both predictable and unpredictable mobilisation use a compact battery of skills
- planning requires sequencing, prioritisation, the exclusion of irrelevant information, an enactment and a conclusion
- even very young children are capable of high order mobilisation of knowledge
- there is a strong relationship between static and mobilised knowledge and the former is fuel for the latter.

COMMUNICATE

Communication is multimodal

To some it might seem strange to list communication as one of four separate headings about knowledge. But it is a unique kind of knowledge. It is the means to encode and decode information. It is the package, not the substance. The goal of all our efforts in education is that students will be able to express what they have learned and what they know, think, feel and imagine.

Communication can be broadly categorised into two domains: verbal and non-verbal. Verbal communication includes oral language, reading and writing. Non-verbal communication includes all body language and gesture, and the expression of ideas through media, movement and materials.

Each type of communication has its own structure, alphabet and vocabulary. Simply put, for music it is the composition, the melody and the notes. For dance it is the form, the choreography and the steps. Whether it is spoken language, painting, movement, sculpture, music or dance, there are central conventions and elements we learn to recognise and respond to in order to understand what is being communicated. The systems for communicating knowledge are separate from knowledge. They are the means to encode and decode knowledge to share it.

If you are conversant with the internationally renowned educational philosophy from Reggio Emilia in northern Italy, you will know that Loris Malaguzzi (the progenitor of the philosophy), saw children as having a hundred languages for expressing themselves.

The child
is made of one hundred.
The child has a hundred languages

a hundred hands
a hundred thoughts
a hundred ways of thinking ...

The poem emphasises the multi-modal nature of communication. Communication is internal, in the mind and the emotions; and external, expressed with the voice and the body. The educators in Reggio Emilia talk about 'the expressive, the communicative and the cognitive languages'.

I believe this is the perfect way to talk about communication. It emphasises the infinite ability of the human mind and body to create forms of expression that enable us to formulate and share our experience and our understanding of the world.

Children express their knowledge using 'words, movement, drawing, painting, building, sculpture, shadow play, collage, dramatic play, or music to name a few' (Edwards, Gandini, & Foreman 1998).

In the early years, the expressive languages should not be thought of as belonging to the curriculum area of art. Rather, this expression, using media, tools and materials, is the child's vehicle for engaging with the world to develop understanding of what it is and how it works. When I outline the learning zones in later chapters, you will see how these expressive languages are leveraged in this way.

As educators we talk about developing students' literacy which usually refers to verbal communication (speaking, reading and writing). But children can become literate in all modes of communication.

There is great diversity in the modes we use to communicate information and meaning: concrete manipulative, photographic, pictorial, graphic, tabular, schematic, symbolic, verbal written, verbal spoken, gestural, postural, locomotor and digital. You are likely to add even more. Students thrive when they learn to decode and encode the structure and elements of each.

For example, the tabular format is highly underestimated. Knowledge of what a column is and what a row is, how the flow of the communication goes from left to right and from the top to the bottom, is assumed, not often overtly explained and understood. It is pivotal for understanding x and y axes later in maths. (Of course, these directions for tables are not the same in all languages.) There are also conventions when interpreting pictures in books, for instance what is above a character is usually interpreted as being spatially behind it. Speech bubbles and thinking bubbles are different.

Decoding and encoding modes of communication

In general, decoding of information is arrived at first. Young children's language learning is exponential. Most often, their receptive language is much stronger than their expressive language. It is important to scaffold and strengthen the progress from receptive to expressive language. There are multiple ways we can achieve this, and they will be explored in detail soon.

If you are yawning as a primary teacher at this point, (I see you!), let me say that this is also true of older children when they are learning new things. It takes a child about 40 repetitions of a word in context before they have genuinely consolidated it. So, even with older students, we need to be aware of developing solid vocabulary, that ensures children not only understand it but can activate and articulate it with the appropriate meaning in the correct context. There is a big divide between receptive understanding and auto-expression of that understanding. Expressive language does not only operate in conversation with others, but is also a stepping stone to children's self-talk, or what we call interior dialogue. Self-talk is a vital component in thinking and learning. Where do you do most of your thinking, planning and problem-solving? (And I'm not talking about in the car or in the shower!)

When children articulate their knowledge, they are encoding. This is a higher level of skill than decoding. They have to come up with and activate the words themselves. This activation of recall is a recognised way that memory is enhanced (Buzan 2010).

A similar gap in skills occurs when children are learning to write. In the same way that receptive language is more advanced than expressive in young children, so too there is a huge gap between what an early primary student can *tell you* and what they can communicate in their writing. If we insist that students write down their ideas, and we don't also give them the opportunity to communicate their knowledge orally, or in non-verbal modalities, we could miss out on about 80% of what they really know or think. So, as we are introducing children to a new mode of communication, it is good practice to allow them to continue using the one they already have a sophisticated grasp of, so that their expression is maximised.

Once students learn the structure, vocabulary and alphabet of different modes, they are in a position to use the rules, or break the rules, to generate unique and creative products. Later we will explore the excellent information on the top-level structures of language as elaborated by Benjamin Bartlett (Bartlett 2003).

Process words: communicating, understanding, recognising, monitoring, assigning meaning, interpreting, decoding, encoding, articulating, expressing.

IN SUMMARY:

- communication is the vehicle for decoding and encoding information
- communication is multimodal and can be divided into verbal and non-verbal areas
- decoding precedes encoding in most cases
- each mode of communication has its own structure, vocabulary and alphabet
- there are central conventions and formats in each type of communication
- we should continue to allow students to use a mode they are proficient in while they are learning a new mode
- once children understand the modes and their structures, they can use them to encode their ideas in unique and creative ways.

Okay, now exhale!

One takeaway from this chapter is the common-sense maxim that high order problem-solving and creativity are built on good foundational knowledge. A second is that you only see what you are looking for. If you expand your horizons, or sharpen your focus, you see more.

I hope that you have a deeper understanding of each foundational knowledge component to support both your planning and your students' learning. I also hope you are highly alert to processes. For your convenience I have included a summary of 12 thinking skills in Part 4 of this book.

What kind of foundational knowledge is your favourite?

What are three things you might do differently after reading this chapter?

Is there something you'd like to share with your colleagues?

CHAPTER 3

Vertical Knowledge – Power Up Your Curriculum GPS

'Would you tell me, please, which way I ought to go from here?'
'That depends a good deal on where you want to get to,'
said the Cat.
'I don't much care where,' said Alice.
'Then it doesn't matter which way you go,' said the Cat.
Lewis Carroll
Alice's Adventures in Wonderland

When you embark on a journey, you load coordinates into your global positioning system. Your destination determines the route. In just this way, when you plan your curriculum, you will have a goal in mind. I indicated that my goal for you, from reading this book, is to feel energised and secure in your knowledge when you plan, implement and assess your curriculum to support concept-based learning. This relates to my vision that all educators are agile and adaptive to get the most out of every learning situation.

Expert planning, implementation and assessment combine to make your communication clear and confident. Parents will trust you, education authorities will cite your work and your centre will be a role model of excellence.

The first thing to clear away is any idea that planning comes first. High achieving educators set goals before they plan. And goals originate from a clear educational vision, born from the question: *what do you want your curriculum to achieve?*

Secondly, planning and assessment are not separate, they are intertwined. Planning is what you project into your context. Assessment is monitoring what happens once it's activated. Planning is not a once-off thing, that happens at the start, and assessment is not a once-off thing that happens at the end. It is a constant to and fro – a dialogue. Sure, you do substantial planning at the outset and you report at the end. But once your plan is enacted, you constantly assess and relaunch the plan.

Until now, the discussion has been focused around concept formation and metacognition – about what is going on inside kids' brains. But we haven't yet looked at the context of content more broadly.

Clearly, you want children to experience a thinking curriculum. Whilst in play, children are constantly thinking, even if that thinking is a kind of sensory monitoring. What are you going to offer students to animate their concept formation and thinking?

There isn't a curriculum document worth its salt that doesn't have statements similar to the ones below.

We offer a comprehensive program.
We care for your child in a nurturing environment.
We build on interests.
We reinforce important concepts.
We offer a customised learning journey for each child.
Your child will become a thoughtful global citizen.
We value and respect diversity.
We develop a play-based learning program.
We value creativity and encourage children to be independent thinkers.

As mentioned, the launching point of your planning is what your vision encompasses and what you tell parents you do.

This book is not about persuading any educator to step away from their philosophy. If a play-based curriculum is what you believe in, then that is what you continue to provide. If your curriculum is called the 'young scientists' program and you favour a structured curriculum, then similarly that is what you will do. Maria Montessori (Montessori 1965) and Rudolf Steiner programs, and several other philosophies developed by pivotal early years' thinkers of their time, are well established and highly regarded.

The information in this book is offered to bolster your own *conceptual and metacognitive understanding* about what you do every minute of every day. It is about you *always recognising the potential to catalyse learning*. As an edu-chameleon, you are constantly and actively making decisions. You recognise opportunities in any situation to propel or pivot learning. Propelling learning is to continue on the same course, powerfully. Pivoting learning is shifting the direction either slightly, or dramatically, to use what is current for a related, or an equally important, but adjusted, goal.

What I have often encountered is that the staff in a centre or school can state their vision, but they may not know exactly how to translate and animate it in their everyday practice. What is a comprehensive program? What is a customised learning journey? How do children increase their understanding of the world within each of these visions?

Mapping the curriculum

Where does content come from? Let's talk about subject areas or disciplines, what I have referred to as vertical knowledge. You might be mandated to, or choose to, include specific subjects in your curriculum. My wish for you is, rather than feel your curriculum is dictated to you, circumscribing you or overwhelming you, that you use it as a reference, to choreograph and design it in your own way. Have a personal point of view. Own it. If you ensure your content across the year is from several disciplines, your work will be balanced and comprehensive. Include your passions. Bring everything you know and love to it. In Reggio Emilia, the educators look widely for inspiration. They reference the work of engineers, architects, poets, artists, designers and more.

Use knowledge, interests and ideas that resonate with you as the stimulus for your design. Then locate your personal focus within the disciplines where they originate and belong. In its discipline, your own interest and idea will connect to a large reservoir of existing and evolving knowledge that you can draw on. It is a point to research from and to plan from. Use it to stretch students' knowledge in that discipline and across disciplines. Something you find fascinating, an artifact, idea, piece of music, can be a provocation. It is the stone thrown into a pond that generates a knowledge ripple effect.

STEM and humanities

As a junior primary teacher, you will have relative certainty about the disciplines and subject areas included in your curriculum. As a preschool teacher you often have carte blanche, and sometimes that breadth of possibility is frightening rather than emancipating!

Selecting content is artfully done bearing the current abilities of the children in the age range you are working with.

Although we know that knowledge goes up in complexity throughout schooling, it is a mistake to see early learning as simple. At the start of my work in preschool, I held what I thought was a logical belief: that play with concrete materials could teach children anything on earth. If only children all played with blocks, surely they would all be good mathematicians! After all, blocks teach them about length, weight, size, shape, colour, balance, density, volume, symmetry, stability, numbers ...

Any book on the value of play will list this type of conceptual learning. But what I didn't realise, was that the learning I was observing was often experiential learning. Some children learn directly as though by osmosis and they might know what all those features are called, but often children need mediation and facilitation to genuinely understand these concepts. As you saw earlier, knowing something is only the beginning. It needs to be connected, stored, mobilised and communicated.

What was missing in my original thoughts was that children had to move beyond the here-and-now to master concepts abstractly. They can know something experientially, but if they aren't able to label it, think about it and transfer it somewhere else, the knowledge is not available for use.

The tiny, landmark book I read which had me refine my ideas was *Children's Minds*, by a student of Piaget, Margaret Donaldson (Donaldson 1984). It revolutionised my educational purpose. I needed to be concerned with children's language learning, their abstract thought, their laying down of foundations, their transfer of knowledge and their innovative ideas.

Beyond the early years, content does become more abstract and complex and the amount of information grows by orders of magnitude. In fact, content is so vast these days that we throw our hands up. There's just too much, we can't teach it all! On top of this, I am sure you have heard it said that it's no longer important to memorise content, because we can look up anything on the internet.

Let's pause for a moment and consider this.

I agree with David Epstein's contention in his book *Range* that, 'You have people walking around with all the knowledge of humanity on their phone, but they have no idea how to integrate it' (Epstein 2019).

Content is the conceptual understanding of how the world works. Understanding is not isolated, random, episodic facts. Understanding is connected facts. To deal with the huge explosion of knowledge, what is required is not Google, it is an internal structure for organising and locating knowledge in the human brain.

If it's not in the brain, or across a few marvellous collaborating brains, it cannot be used to fuel problem-solving or creativity. The idea is to have stored concepts that connect to more and more general categories. A bird falls in a category aves, and along with other animals in the broader area of zoology, which is part of the life sciences, which are part of the general sciences. When it is located, it can be cross-pollinated and integrated with other high order knowledge. Google comes in at the point where you know that some of your knowledge is missing and you embark on research. That's when you reach out into that amazing network, the world wide web. Find others who are searching for new answers like you and synthesise knowledge in new ways or invent new thinking and ideas.

Children need subject knowledge and they also need to know how it is expressed or communicated. Every discipline, at its foundation, is about literacy. I have never (and I'm sure you haven't either) come across a subject where we don't encounter specialised knowledge. Just as we must learn how to speak a foreign language, we must also learn how to speak maths, computer science, music, dance, law, and every other subject. Each discipline also has its own structural forms, vocabulary and alphabet. And many have specific units of measurement to provide precision and accuracy in its communication.

We can journey towards our curriculum destination packing a trunk containing only one subject, or we can load a couple of disciplines to enrich the journey.

A confluence of paths

There is a dialogue in the early years, about children developing fluid knowledge. In the 21st century, more than ever, hybrid knowledge is where innovation originates – think 3D animations in medicine (WEHImovies 2020). Digital communication and science together, make it possible for the medical world to see human and other life forms' cross-sections, systems and micro-details in a way that has never been possible before.

Inter-disciplinary content is quite difficult to achieve higher up in education because subjects may be taught in silos by different teachers. For their work to cross over, they need to actively collaborate amongst themselves. An inspiring film, *Most Likely to Succeed* describes how this was done in a high school in San Diego, USA (Whitely 2015).

In the early years' arena, educators have a wonderful opportunity to integrate disciplines when they plan their content. If we understand each discipline, we can overtly choose the ones we want to harness and use together. When I want to position content, I think of the traditional sciences, and humanities.

We regularly see this vertical knowledge classification:

- Science
- Technology
- Engineering
- Mathematics
- The Arts
- History
- Languages
- Literacy
- Philosophy
- Law
- Ethics

How is the overview of disciplines useful to us?

In short, the list is STEM plus the humanities. For balance, we plan a curriculum which includes knowledge from a range of disciplines and implement it at the appropriate level remembering Vygotsky's zone of proximal development. Schools generally calibrate how balanced their subjects are in their scope and sequence across year levels. But occasionally I have seen children do dinosaurs or hatch chicken eggs three or four times in their early education. You see law, philosophy and ethics in the list. There are ways to include these in your work. After all, what are the rules in your classroom? Who made them? Are they fair? What happens when someone breaks them? How do you make collaborative decisions? What can you do as a group for others?

High level questions as gateways to discipline knowledge

With such an array of content and so many disciplines available, how do we make them accessible? The International Baccalaureate Organisation's Primary Years Program (IBO 2020) has masterminded accessibility by formulating simple but profound overarching questions that open gates to the disciplines we have listed. Their curriculum asks:

- Who are we?
- Where are we in place and time?
- How do we express ourselves?
- How does the world work?

I love a question as an entrance to knowledge, because it suggests that we research and act to reach answers. I think the overarching questions are valuable and highly flexible entry points to discipline knowledge, and we can immediately see how 'knowing who we are' prompts us to think about our personal, communal and cultural identity. 'Where we are in place and time', suggests geography, history and more. If your centre has a religious or philosophical framework included in its vision, you might frame a complementary overarching question to open doors to that understanding. It is important to state here, that an overarching question asking us to understand our identity, relates to past, current and future perspectives. More and more our curricula ask us to engage with who we and our students are as enactors and generators of the future.

Onboarding your co-travellers

So now you've chosen subject areas and selected concept rich content you want to cover. What's next?

Early in my career, I was made to feel intensely incompetent when a new teacher arrived with 46 boxes of plans, materials and resources – a box for every week of the school year! I was rabidly jealous. She was SO organised! She had delivered the same curriculum for the past eight years and counting.

I have learnt a lot since then!

If you go ahead and enact your plan exactly as it is, you are limiting its potential. Your students' role needs to be accommodated if you are genuinely interested in their reciprocity, motivation and interest.

With us, without us, or despite us, children are active learners who constantly construct their own theories about how the world works. If they are institutionally ignored, what they learn is that it's not worth the effort to offer a suggestion.

Some educators might counter this notion of attending to young children's theories citing that they are often incorrect, unscientific or, frankly, untrue. Of course, this may be the case. But the intention is not to leave children in partial understanding or ignorance. Rather it is to help them accumulate evidence in the world around them to refine and develop their ideas through a series of provisional theories. By providing experiences, and materials to challenge them; by offering media and methods for communication and ongoing dialogue, we journey with them to conceptual clarity and creativity. When we do this, we usually discover that they have perspectives, wisdom or reveal imagination we hardly believed possible.

Loris Malaguzzi said:

'All people – and I mean scholars, researchers and teachers who in any place have set themselves to study children seriously – have ended up by discovering not so much the limits and weaknesses of children but rather their surprising and extraordinary strengths and capabilities linked with an inexhaustible need for expression and realisation.'

In the next chapter, I will discuss a project called 'Explorations' to unpack ways to unify curriculum goals and plans with children's ideas, motivations and discoveries.

But for now, I want to turn to assessment.

How is the journey going?

Earlier you read that planning is what you project into your curriculum content and assessment is monitoring what happens once it's activated.

Pedagogy of listening

In 2000, I made my first of three study tours to Reggio Emilia. One of the lectures by Carla Rinaldi reframed assessment as 'a pedagogy of listening' (Rinaldi 2001). When I heard her address on listening, it was the first time I truly recognised my value as an early childhood educator.

The listening she describes uses all the educator's intellectual and affective faculties, not just their ears. The pedagogy of listening is respectful, hears back, gives time, is multimodal, sensitive, reflective, curious, conscious of emotion, suspends judgement, and most movingly 'removes the individual from anonymity'.

These ideas are much less declarative than anything I have written so far in this book. This makes sense, because I can declare my own knowledge, as can you. I know my plan, but I honestly never know what I am listening for from children until I hear it. I can *anticipate* much of what I will hear back from assessment, but I know that I will always be surprised, excited, concerned, validated, stumped, humbled, amused, delighted and so much more. Because every child is unique! We *don't* know everything about them.

When I am assessing, I am listening for more than intellectual knowledge. I am observing the relationships children have with their peers. Observing levels of motivation. Perseverance is on my radar. Not that I would insist that a child stick to some task beyond where frustration kicks in, but I want to extend it over time. I am checking to see whether they rely on the same friends, materials and activities each day, so I can slightly challenge that and introduce some flexibility. I am watching for independence in negotiating the room, how stable or variable moods are. How they deal with conflict. And I know that you are too when you are in the observer/evaluator role. These observations collectively cross several areas. They relate to what Art Costa (Costa 2008) calls habits of mind, or what Daniel Goleman (Goleman 1995) characterises as emotional intelligence.

We are listening, for:

- Who is this child?
- How are they thinking, discovering, acting, communicating?
- What is their relationship with the group?
- How is he or she interpreting the world?

When we ask these questions, we are searching, or researching. We also ask questions about ourselves. As secure as we think we are in our knowledge, research is being open. The research is about the process of learning, relationships, seeing possibility, finding new meaning, seeing links, experiencing highlights, finding nodes of interest, unpacking values, surfacing beliefs, recognising change, feeling emotion and seeing how everything is resonating together.

'Hang on a minute,' I hear you say. 'This book is about concepts and you are hammering on about affect and emotion, motivation and resilience. Isn't that another book?'

It is crucial to state that if we want conceptual understanding, we *have to* be aware of affect. Piaget and Reuven Feuerstein both saw affect and cognition as two sides of the same coin. This means that children can metacognitively review and understand their emotions, moods, energy and application to a task through a thinking rather than a feeling lens. If it is only feeling, they have no way to either understand or transform their behaviour. If it is a thinking lens, they have the scope to pause, reflect and review. Affect and thought are both harnessed in great concept learning.

With all our senses, and through both cognitive and affective lenses, we tune into what is happening successfully, or what is running well. Our evaluation enables us to change course if interest wanes, or find new resources to keep learning on track. Occasionally, this alertness might mean we have to design a new destination. But mostly, it means discovering the path that is most meaningful and engaging to our students. There are many roads to Rome, or indeed, to punctuation!

Finding the optimal engagement is a tightrope, between not scaffolding children's understanding of the world enough, and inundating them with prescriptive ideas that don't motivate or inspire them. Evaluation, listening and assessing are what enables you to balance on the rope. In many seminars I've presented over time, teachers start off thinking assessment is the hardest and most frustrating part of their role – then they end up loving it the most!

In a later chapter, I will talk more about taming your assessment avalanche by clarifying your focus. I will also talk about managing the capture, recording, storage and flexible use of your observations.

Orientation provides different points of view

When you use the knowledge GPS to map your balanced curriculum, you need to be aware of differing points of view. In our role, we deal with so many vying stakeholders: government, education departments, leadership, colleagues, parents, students, specialists, the broader community and ... the media. There will be disparate and even opposing points of view. You will, hopefully, be guided by the vision and philosophy of your school or centre regarding how it positions itself. No matter what you include in your curriculum, you will be cognisant of these points of view and you will be applying considerate filters. We must be aware of the social, ethical and philosophical dialogues around inclusion, culture, religion family circumstances and gender. It is extremely important. As educators we are role models for the whole community. What I'd like to suggest is not to make the points of view the content, but to approach the content in a way that is respectful to the points of view.

> ## IN SUMMARY:
>
> - it is useful to have an overview of the disciplines from which our curricula are drawn and designed
> - there are two overarching categories: STEM and humanities
> - all the disciplines are underpinned by language and literacy
> - high level questions are gateways or access points to subject areas
> - we need children to experience a balance of disciplines over time, so a scope and sequence is desirable
> - assessment is the art of listening with all senses and with both intellect and affect to what is running well and to note what children are learning, how they are interacting in social engagements and how they navigate the educational environment
> - we need to ensure we are respectful of cultural, ethical, religious and gender issues.

CHAPTER 4

Distributed Knowledge

I therefore suggest that we should focus on the greatest source of variance that can make the difference – the teacher.
John Hattie

Everyone needs habits of mind that allow them to dance across disciplines.
David Epstein
Range: How Generalists Triumph in a Specialized World

We have had a look at foundational, vertical and distributed knowledge in Chapter 2. I would like to briefly revisit it here to demonstrate the relationships between vertical and distributed knowledge. Vertical knowledge is what the world knows; and distributed knowledge is how we engage with that extant knowledge. You will note that when you plan content, you draw knowledge from different disciplines in the vertical knowledge domain. So, this graphic is titled trans-disciplinary learning. How you deploy and elaborate that knowledge with children is up to you. You calibrate its energy, democracy, depth and range.

You will note the representation in the distributed knowledge domain of the closed-ended and open-ended systems. These have already been prefigured and will be discussed in detail further along in the discourse.

I started off talking about three kinds of knowledge because I wanted to keep it simple. But here I will introduce a fourth kind: cyclical knowledge.

Existing vertical knowledge does not remain static. In fact, we are responsible for transforming what is known through our own learning, research, innovation and action. What we discover feeds back into vertical knowledge.

There is also a relationship between closed and open-ended systems. We, and students, use what we know to fuel creativity, and creativity gives us new formulas and rules to develop improved closed-ended systems. The following section is a discussion about how knowledge occurs within the curriculum and elaborates the themes of closed- and open-ended practice already discussed in the section on foundational knowledge.

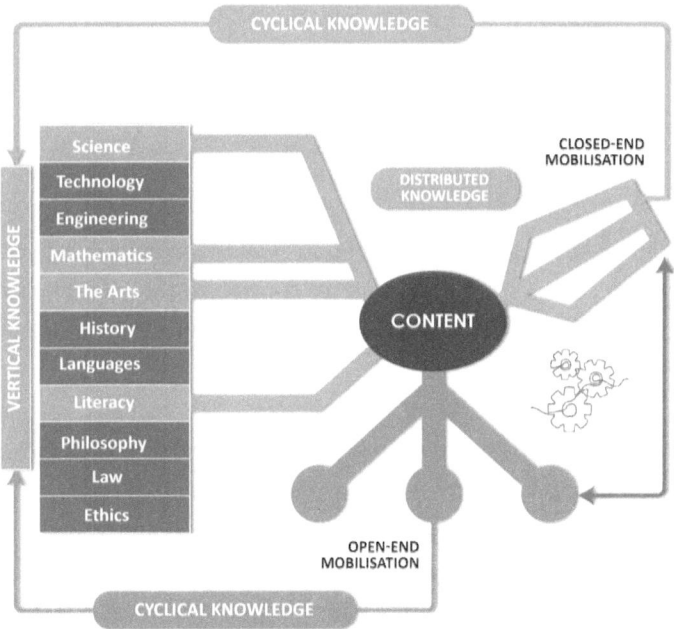

Figure 9: Trans-disciplinary learning

The dancer and the dance

You are the choreographer of your curriculum. As choreographer you arrange the dance. But you also give over the dance to the dancers.

I alerted you that I would share in this chapter the 'Explorations Project' to get a picture of how children's interests can be included within your plan in an authentic way. I chose this project to discuss with you because it originated in a middle school setting as a collaborative exploration of the four elements: earth, fire, water and air. The year fives were in a 'buddy' program with the preschool where I was the director and teaching a four-year-old group for three days a week. I loved the explorations idea and was inspired to mirror it in our centre. The content is suitable for both primary and preschool students. The year fives did all four elements, and we chose 'air' for the three-year-olds and 'water' for the fours.

Dancing with projects

Our preschool program was designed to include projects. But if you don't use a project-based methodology, try and relate the pivotal processes for activating children's thinking in the examples below to how you could use them in your context.

Projects can be long and transdisciplinary, or short, sharp and limited in scope. It is easy to reframe some of what is happening in play-based learning as investigative projects. An important point to make, is that our program was not exclusively based on projects. We designed a learning environment with a variety of play and learning spaces. Home or themed fantasy play corner, communication table, table-top activities, art easel, collage table, sand trays, inquiry displays, reading and book corner. I am sure you recognise all of these. Incidentally, early primary classrooms are often set up with the same flexibility and opportunities for large group, small group and individual experiences.

In the preschool setting, we usually have the amazing luxury of two adults in the room. Over the years I devised metaphors for our roles. During the day one of us acted as a microscope, spending time with a small group for a purpose we had planned and resourced; and the other, acted as radar, roving and documenting with photos or notes, directing, supporting, scaffolding, resourcing or observing the whole group. I particularly love the radar role, because you are alert for what is current in the room as the children engage with one another and with materials.

In primary settings, where two adults are rare in one group, I have seen very successful team teaching. Two and even three teachers across a year level, plan together and allocate children to different activities across a single or even multiple spaces. This often leaves at least one teacher available to be the radar.

We would customise the arrangement of the room to suit a current project. Certain areas would be activated and resourced specifically to underpin the central ideas of the project. We didn't expect every child to be involved in the central project all the time. Students flowed in an out of it. For some important skills or knowledge, we made a list and did want everyone to use a material or interpret an idea. This was often how we gathered data on levels of knowledge and skill development.

Sometimes we commenced a project, paused, and picked up the threads later. Children astounded me with their incredible memory of projects, especially how their own or other children's ideas had been included. I once did a project across prep and year one, where children authored collaborative books based on an author study of Leo Lionni. Where I taught at the time, the teacher had two years with the same students. When the children started their book, they couldn't read or write. They told the stories orally and illustrated them. Two years later, at a book launch, they stood at a podium and read their book aloud to an audience of over 80 parents and grandparents. Children have memories like elephants!

The 'Explorations' project was about a single feature in the world: water. We took a single idea and broadened it out. At other times, our projects were more general, with titles like 'Taking Time', 'Body Talk', 'Our Place in Space' and 'Line Dance' which was an exploration of how lines work in the world. In these projects we started with a broad idea and explored what was within it. And we always left space for mini projects, unrelated to the main project to unravel into action.

After that meander into projects more generally, let's get back to 'Explorations'. When the decision was made to embark on it, I did what I always do, and developed a massive mind map of ideas related to water. I asked my colleagues to do the same. But I was also interested in what parents and grandparents might bring to the project, so I sent out a newsletter and asked them, if they were interested, to share their ideas about what water meant to them.

I was inundated with responses.

Many of the ideas matched what we'd set out already, but there were some wonderful new perspectives, like information about water engineering from a father involved in sanitation. We also included indigenous perspectives and some dreamtime stories, including that of the 'Rainbow Serpent', who in some versions, created waterways, and these were narrated by an elder invited to our centre.

Among the disciplines included were:

- physics: the states of water (liquid, solid, gas)
- life sciences: water as sustaining life
- urban planning: water reticulation
- geography: landforms related to water (valleys, lakes, river systems, estuaries and the ocean)
- the arts: photography, painting, pen and ink drawing, narrative, drama, music and dance.

Giving the dance over to the dancers

Here are two stories, which both harnessed children's interests. The first is about a 'water-moving machine'. I include it, because it is a situation where I and my colleagues had all the knowledge to solve problems for children but stood back and allowed them to do it on their own. This is an instance of closed-ended mobilisation and problem-solving towards a predicable conclusion.

The second is about a 'water dance'. Here, once again, standing back was an excellent option. The dance project as you will see, is an example of mobilising knowledge with open-ended and unknown outcomes. We've talked about that as imagination and creativity.

The water-moving machine

A child, Lewis, told me he wanted to make a water-moving machine.
'How amazing,' I said, 'do you know what it will look like?'
'Yes,' said Lewis.

He wanted to move water from one side of the sandpit to the other. The equipment available included two plastic pipes about 1.5m in length with different diameters, so one fit inside the other, but not snugly.

He laid them out in the sandpit, one partially inside the other, collected a bowl of water and tried to pour some into one side of the two-pipe structure. Of course, trying to pour water into pipes horizontal to the sand, with one cylinder being wider was, to put it mildly, hopeless. Several children got involved in the problem-solving. They also had trouble trying to pour water into the pipes. The water was just dribbling out at the entrance to the pipe and being absorbed into the sand at the source.

Just before the end of play one child said, 'We have to lift it up!' (Conceptual breakthrough!)

Once inside, Lewis shared his plan and his problems. We suggested that anyone interested could draw the machine. The child who'd made the suggestion to raise the pipes up, drew them slanting down from a support, a big wooden reel she knew we had in the garden. The concepts involved here relate to position and direction. The pipe had to be placed at an incline to ensure the gravitational downward flow of water.

Another child, who's mind had obviously been ticking over, showed us he'd drawn the water being poured into the 'machine' with a watering can. This addressed the conceptual problem of dimension. The children had been trying to pour water into the mouth of the pipe using several less accurate vessels and water was being spilled before entering the pipe. They agreed the watering can was much better than the ineffectual bowl they had been using. They used these conceptual improvements to refine their drawings.

The next day, we marched out to the sandpit with a mission. They got all the equipment together.

But it wasn't plain sailing. They encountered issues keeping the pipes on the big reel. They also had to lock the inner pipe into place by pushing some cloth between it and the pipe containing it. They had to bolster the two-pipe unit up halfway along (concept of stability).

Eventually after multiple attempts, the watering can poured water along the slanted pipes to the other side of the sandpit. Gravity, inclines and managing flow had worked for them.

After all that, the water was just seeping into the sand at the opposite end! They had to work out a way of collecting the water. In a brainwave, a plastic container was produced, and the supplier explained that it didn't leak because it wasn't 'sorbent' like the sand.

Through a combination of planning, experimenting, drawing and refining the drawings, they had solved several conceptual physics problems. It couldn't be explained verbally from the start. When the originator of the idea and his friends drew and reflected on the problems, they were able to progress the solutions. The machine's efficiency was developed using different modalities, concrete manipulation, thinking, drawing, trial and error. The children were on the verge of explaining the concept of 'pressure' because they were aware that the flow needed to be constant for the water to continue moving through the pipes. This was a short, related project.

Figure 10: The Water moving machine

Water dance

One day, when we were still involved in the explorations project, Matilda turned up with a program from 'The Nutcracker' ballet.

How would you respond?

You could honour her interest by engaging in a brief conversation and acknowledge her generosity in sharing it with you. Or you might give her time to tell the group about it and ask her to place it on an investigation table.

Park it.

You can keep it parked – *and sometimes that is the best decision*, because to follow the lead, you need to expend time and effort, which are finite commodities. You need to ensure that, if you progress the idea, there is value for her, the individual child, and for the group.

You decide to use it to elevate children's learning.

The ballet program is an artefact. It is located in performance arts. It is also a specific format of communication. How do you include the artefact in your curriculum? You consider what else the ballet program might be connected to? Perhaps there is a multi-cultural celebration soon, and the national dances in 'The Nutcracker' dovetail into the planning for that?

In my case, the year five students happened to be creating a 'Water Dance' on the middle school campus as part of their exploration. So, I organised for them to come across and perform it for our groups.

Our kids immediately wanted to do their own dance.

As stated, the ballet program links to performance arts and literacy. But why stop at two disciplines? This is the secret of transdisciplinary learning.

They began. They liked the idea of a water dance, but it had to include the hip-hop 'worm' some of them were obsessed with. No pirouettes. Surprise! Not everyone is a balletomane like me! They spent time experimenting and making up their steps for the dance. There were a lot of flowing waves and spirals, and the worms were water droplets popping into a pool! We had provided photographs of different patterns of water, like concentric circles, waves, droplets, etc.

These photographs were also the source of some exceptional water pattern paintings. I have a digital montage of them displayed in my home! I have included four of them here, because they are suggestive of the dance steps the children created for their dance.

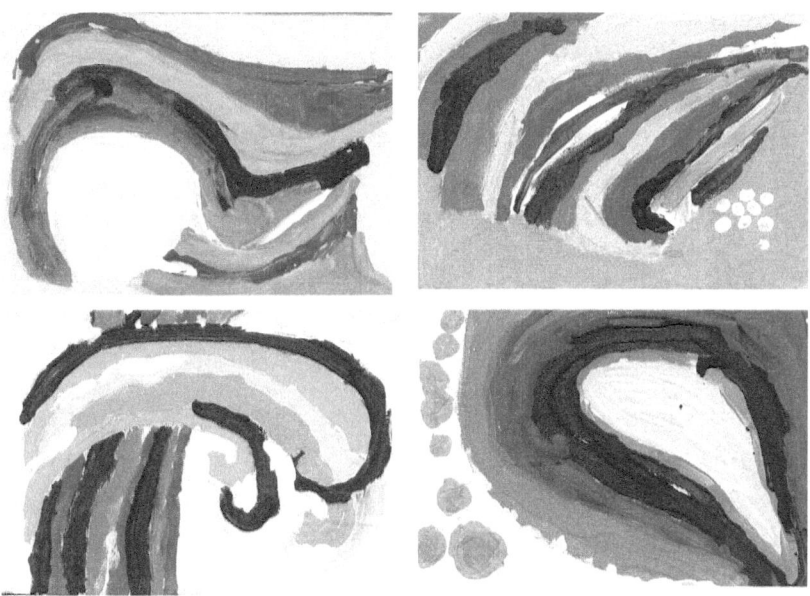

Figure 11: Water pattern paintings – 4-year-old children

We resourced the children with time, space, writing and art materials to represent the dance. It was not a drawing of dancers.

They invented a symbol system for each step and recorded the sequence of steps. Then they recorded how many repetitions there were of each sequence in the structure. They negotiated. They assigned roles, refined the choreography, practised, organised the costumes, created a program, invited everyone, planned the seating, planned the menu, and finally got to perform for an audience of parents.

The artefact mobilised open-ended creativity. By the end of the project, they had used formats and units of measurement from literacy, geometric and numerical mathematics and the performance arts. Their agency was intact and there was tremendous collaborative planning and action.

These are all things we are counselled to ensure children are capable of when they navigate the world independently. It is no accident that the students created a symbol system for their dance, or that they counted the sequences in the structure to record them. Much of this was *choreographed* by asking them questions, providing materials, asking refining questions. Children don't have to be told what to do, they can respond to scaffolding, finely tuned prompts and facilitation.

I know what you mean

What was my purpose in having the children represent their ideas using their own diagrams and symbols? It was so that they themselves encoded information into modes that can be interpreted by others. Did their uncle Ed understand the symbols? Most likely not, but *they* did. They had agreed on what the symbols meant.

And that is what is happening in the world in all disciplines all the time. People are agreeing about what signs mean. Even as we invent new technologies, like digital modes and coding, the languages have to be precise and communicable.

For instance, in maths, there is this squiggly sign, π.

Laying down foundations for later learning

Each discipline has specific content. But it also has characteristic, universally agreed formats and modes of communication. Literature has poems, maths has equations, science has experiments, dance has pas de deux and pirouettes ... and worms! Some disciplines also have definitive units of measurement. To master these subjects, students will be required to master specialised forms, symbols and terminology.

When the children create their own symbols, they are learning about multimodal communication. And their learning is active, not passive.

When do you serve your pi?

Pi is one of the most well-known mathematical constants representing the ratio of a circle's circumference to its diameter. For any circle, the distance around the edge is a little more than three times the distance across. And pi (3.141592654) is one of literally hundreds of symbols children will have to learn to interpret and remember as they navigate the subject. They need a conceptual understanding of the symbol.

We are not going to teach pi in preschool, or early primary. But to understand it, length is important. Children can use string to surround a circle, cut it and then unwind it. It's a reference and can be compared to the string from a bigger, equal or smaller circle. Pi can't be understood without this first step – measuring the circumference of a circle. (We don't use the word 'circumference'. But be ready for the child who might!)

To understand pi, they will also need to know what a diameter is. And a ratio.

Ratio and proportion, *without using the terminology*, can be investigated with a wide range of hands-on experiences in the early years.

Understanding 'more', 'the same' and 'less' is what we are always doing in mathematics.

'Look at the water in this glass, I wonder, if we pour it into that jar, will it be more than half, or less than half?'

'I wonder which block weighs more?'

'Oh, you have discovered that the big block weighs the same as these two blocks together! So, we need two blocks on one side of the scale to balance the big block there. It's two small to one big. (2:1) What if we have two big blocks?'

We don't serve pi up too early, but we begin to develop the *foundational understanding* so that later, they are the kids who get it.

In the same way, when you do geography, you need to understand how to represent topography or weather systems. Again, I'm not suggesting that you teach every child isobars and contour lines! Contour lines are interesting, because the closer they are together, the steeper the slope they represent. We don't teach it, but perhaps, as for the water-moving machine and the water dance, we offer children the opportunity to create their own drawings to represent steep and not steep. If they invent ways to represent their ideas, theories and concepts in drawings, diagrams, maps, plans, models, measurements and symbols, it tunes them in to how they will encounter knowledge later. It enhances our agility if we bear in mind the kind of multimodal communication contained in different subjects. Children are not there yet, nor do they need to be. But they are moving towards it.

Early individualistic representation will give way over time to more universal formats, symbols and units and they are introduced during schooling. They might even discover for themselves that communication is useless unless everyone understands it. Or that you can't use something arbitrary to measure with precision.

One of the pivotal projects from the Diana School in Reggio Emilia is called: 'The Shoe and the Meter'. A book has been written about it. It explores the process preschool children go through to reach an agreed unit of measurement when they discover that different shoes do not measure things precisely enough (Castagnetti & Vecchi 1997). The project is a negotiation and exploration about understanding the importance of universally agreed units. The actual brass metre referred to in the book can be visited in the city of Reggio Emilia.

You might be thinking that if you waited for children to create their own units first or discover everything in the world on their own all the time, you'd go nuts! And I agree! *You can't do it all the time*. However, when planning, you can look for opportunities for children to have the idea, then problem-solve their way through the frustration, challenge, discussion and negotiation, and discover the steps to reach a solution. You can also be on the lookout for moments in your incidental interactions with children where you can frame things as a wondering or a brief investigation, rather than a direct answer. But most of all, you can be in awe of what children will encode and learn from it.

What are your three takeaways from this chapter?

Is there an idea that particularly appealed to you?

What might you try in your context after reading this chapter?

IN SUMMARY:

- we can integrate learning from more than one discipline when we design content
- we can work from an individual artefact to the discipline, or work from the discipline, through sub-content to ideas and artefacts
- each discipline has its unique structure, concepts, vocabulary, alphabet, and often, units of measurement
- children benefit from encoding their own ideas and concepts in multi-modal ways as a means of recording their own ideas and concepts
- curriculum engages children when we honour and authentically integrate their interests for the benefit of the individual child and for the group.

CHAPTER 5

Concept Transfer – Crossing the Bridge

An individual understands a concept, skill, theory, or domain of knowledge to the extent that he or she can apply it appropriately in a new situation.
Howard Gardner (Gardner, The Disciplined Mind, 2000)

I am sure that one of your greatest wishes, is that one day your students will say that one of the most important things they learned, they learned from you. An aha moment, an insight, and an inspiration, or even better a string of them, that made a difference in their lives. The best knowledge is a thread that endures, that stays the course through upheavals and transformations. As I write this, our family is in lockdown. We are in the middle of the global COVID crisis. Three of us are in Victoria, and one interstate, unable to fly anywhere. We Victorians are restricted in travel with a limit of a 5km radius and a 9.00pm curfew. In my whole life, I never anticipated this situation. We have had to adapt our expectations, relaunch our ways of communicating, imagine new ways of connecting emotionally, design new ways to enact our professional roles. We have to take what we know from the situation before, adapt and redesign. Taking what we know from one context and adapting it to suit a new context, is transfer. Without it, we would have a hard time dealing with change. And we know that the only certain thing about life, is that it will change.

Transfer is a key goal of successful teaching

As referred to earlier, with the explosion of knowledge, we need to find an approach that enables students to 'use their knowledge across situations' (Darling-Hammond et al. 2008).

In any course about education, we are trained that 'transfer' is an important goal to achieve. Students need to internalise the information we are presenting and then be able to leverage that information elsewhere. This is much more difficult and complex than it sounds.

Unless we structure our teaching to focus on and demonstrate transfer, only some of the students will do it. There are students who are able think laterally and apply what they know in different contexts, but not all students do it. It can't be left to chance.

Transfer implies that a student understands something in a current situation and can perceive how it is related to other objects and situations. Or, they are in a novel situation, and they can import either information or skills from a prior to the new one. Their knowledge is built from a conceptual understanding. They understand the patterns and relationships and can apply them across many contexts and even across disciplines.

Learning to understand relationships in-depth, facilitates subsequent transfer (Darling-Hammond et al. 2008).

There are two kinds of transfer depending on how similar the tasks are:

- near transfer: transfer of knowledge between similar contexts
- far transfer: transfer of knowledge between dissimilar contexts.

For transfer to occur, children must first develop a deep and complete understanding of something in its original context. If the initial learning (particularly if it's something a little complex) isn't consolidated, there is less chance it will be available as a reference point in a new context. Deep knowledge, structural knowledge, not surface knowledge is what facilitates transfer (Meadows 1993).

A motif throughout this book is that organising knowledge is important. When we do this, we take something in the immediate here and now, like me typing on this computer, and link it to other things to contextualise this activity. I am engaged in a recognised convention for communication. In another example, if a child is learning about the plus sign, and they don't learn exactly what the plus sign represents, they are limited to using it to do the specific sum they are working on in that specific moment. They need to go from the particular to the general.

This difference between the specific and the general is something that you, the teacher, knows well. But even if we educators know it, we might not actually plan for the shift between the two to happen.

Spend time at the entrance to the bridge

There is a process for learning something new. One secret is to make sure the first contacts are long and deep enough – and another, is that there isn't interference while it is being learned. A prompt here is that later, when you read about the zone of concept clarity, this information will be very relevant.

I have made the error of introducing the terms vertical and horizontal at the same time. I thought it would be simple because they both referred to positions in space and I assumed kids couldn't possibly confuse standing up and lying down? They didn't confuse the positions, but they did confuse the terminology. 'Hold up your hands to the ceiling, what do we call this?' Half the kids yell vertical, the other half yell horizontal.

Uh oh.

Present information bytes on their own first. Consolidate. Then, before going on to the opposite or different information, provide bytes that are the same, or partially similar. Even if there are elements that are different, *concentrate on what is the same as the original byte* in the new information field. Once that is done well, then select to focus on difference.

Andreas Hansen in his work on concept-based learning, presents a three-part process for learning a new concept (Hansen 2014):

- selective association: concentrating on what is the same or similar
- selective discrimination: concentrating on what is different
- selective generalisation: knowing the concepts so well that you can focus on several similarities and differences in a complex field.

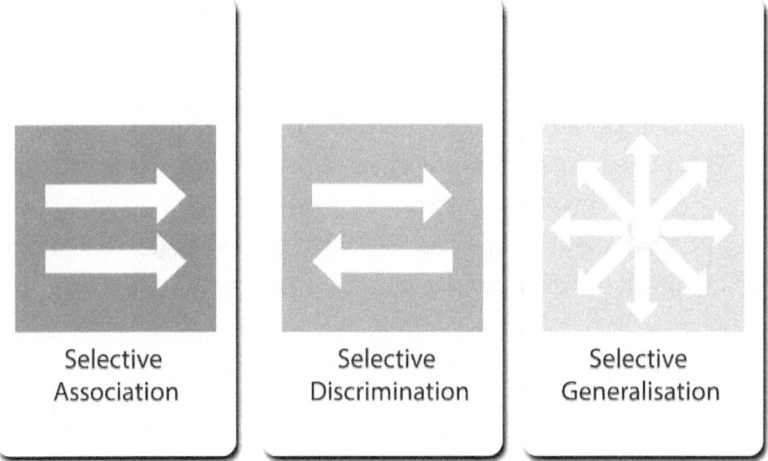

Figure 12: Three phases of concept learning

I will use the introduction to the concept of a rectangle to elucidate this process. But you can substitute any concept for the rectangle. Two dimensional linear shapes are fairly easy to grasp, but imagine introducing fractions! You will see through the process below, that when learning fractions, sticking to one concept, like a half, is better than trying to introduce too many fraction variables at the same time.

Selective association

When it comes to concept-based learning, selective association is the one you spend the most time on, and it has three stages:

1. The first is to genuinely understand the entity you're introducing and its features. Spend time unpacking them with children and supplying them with the appropriate language and labels. So, if we are introducing a rectangle, you will talk about the *number* of sides, the shape of the *angle* or the corners, the *straightness* of the lines. The italicised words refer to the features.

2. During the second stage of association, you compare the focus entity to other things with the same or similar features; *but stay in the immediate context first*. You slightly broaden the concept within a close transfer field. For example, from your box of beautiful tessellation shapes, you arrange some rectangles on the desktop. Children are asked to find the exact match. When they can do this, they might be challenged to find one a different colour, or size, but still a rectangle.

   Then explore the concept in the classroom (not all on the same day necessarily). Look at illustrations, and 3D blocks pointing out the rectangles. Don't call the 3D block a prism yet, the rectangle is a partial similarity, because it is a 2D rectangular face of the block. As part of the second stage, you will ask children if they know where rectangles might exist that are beyond their sensory perception. Where are there rectangles in your home?

   'I know, my fridge!'

   'My front doormat.'

   'Hazelnut chocolate bar!' (No, they did not say that.)

   'The back flap that lifts up on my yellow dump truck that goes with the digger and the concrete mixer.'

   These images challenge them to create a *mental picture* of the shape and fuels their ability to transfer the concept in the future.

3. The third stage of selective association is to have children create their own examples of the concept. Self-production, as we have seen, is about encoding. This can be very creative. You might ask the children to start a drawing with a rectangle and

then turn it into something else, or provide collage materials with rectangles of different sizes, to create a design. This can be done so that they work out that four little ones make up one big one, etc. You can do rectangles outside, create human rectangular formations, etc.

You will know they've got it when a parent says, 'I had no idea there were so many rectangles at my house, and the swimming pool and the supermarket! Now his little sister is collecting them too!'

Selective discrimination

After selective association, move on to selective discrimination – but don't go too far too soon! When introducing the next shape from a rectangle, start with a square, as it shares the features of right-angled corners and straight lines. Emphasise the number of lines, the length of the lines and the shape of the angles. Then, once they've grasped these features, the road is open to triangles. You can later revert to the rectangle and broaden the discussion to quadrilaterals, where the corners are not right angles. As you progress, always aim to introduce the logical next challenge.

Young children may not know what a right angle is, or understand 90 degrees, but they can learn to visually recognise this specific corner. You might join two strips of paper with a split pin and allow them to walk around the room opening the angle of the two strips to match corners on the edge of tables.

The process for deep understanding is to fully understand the features of something and how they change from one universal shape (or other concept) to another.

If children know about a pentagon, and know it's called that because of its five corners, even if they don't know the name for an octagon yet, they might be able to provide their own near accurate name for it – an 'eightagon' perhaps. They understand the *structural ideas* that are constant across different examples. Some elements remain the same (conservation of constancy) and some change. And children can identify and track both.

Selective generalisation

Once the student understands the conservation of constancy of a particular feature, they will be able to manipulate information about both similarities and differences across different contexts. They can choose, in any context, what is similar or different and to what degree they are similar or different.

When we learn a new concept, we go through the following seven steps:

1. Label and understand features of an entity within a context
2. Relate it to identical entities or those with partial similarities in the immediate context
3. Extend the transfer field to more general instances of the concept within a near locale
4. Predict or imagine the entity in a place beyond the locale and where it is not accessible to the senses
5. Encode the entity in self-production tasks
6. Distinguish how the feature changes in another example
7. Be able to recognise similarities and differences in focal features in a complex field.

When we have mediated children through association, discrimination and generalisation, we can challenge them to recognise, categorise, compare, export, reapply and create using their detailed understanding of concepts. You can mix it up. And that gives them the practice they need to identify, apply and activate the concepts elsewhere (to transfer).

While I have used a maths example (the rectangle), this process for concept acquisition is equally valid for a format of writing, a punctuation mark, a landform or a staccato. It is even more important when the content is complex. Fractions, decimals, percentages, ratios, proportions, all have a structural foundation. They are all different ways of explaining part of a confined range, a whole.

In this range, 20%, one fifth, .2, 1:5, are all related. If students understand the structural concept of proportion, they will have less difficulty seeing how these symbolic representations are proportionally the same.

Transporting principles across the bridge

Figure 13: Transfer of bridged concepts

Over the last seven years I have become a trainer in Feuerstein Instrumental Enrichment (FIE) (Feuerstein Institute 2020). This does not mean I have studied music! The instruments are aimed at elucidating particular cognitive functions. Feuerstein methodology packages transfer into every teaching engagement with students. At some time during each encounter, the teacher mediates students' thinking and together, they come up with a generalisable *principle* from the learning.

For instance, the principle (or general statement) might be any of the following:

- for a shape to be a square, it needs four corners connected by four equal straight lines
- if I focus well, I am more able to understand the task I am doing
- if I face a different way, what is on my left and on my right will change
- when I start a task, I need to gather all the information.

The first relates to content (the features of a square), the second to self-regulation (it is dispositional), the third elucidates personal perspective in spatial relations, and the fourth emphasises that there are steps in a procedure and having all the data is step one.

When we create a universal principle, the information is generalised and so is readily packaged to be used in another context. It can be transported across a bridge. At home, the child is asked to go to a cupboard and bring back the square cake tin. He or she knows exactly what to look for and does not bring back a rectangular one.

When the student is in a different classroom with a different teacher approaching a task in a different discipline, they can say the mantra: 'If I focus well, I am more able to understand the task I am doing'. In developing the principle, they have been made aware of self-regulation; and that it can be efficient or inefficient.

Without that awareness, they act out a pattern they have no conscious control over. Recognising, being in touch with their feelings or attitudes towards learning, is being mindful about it.

They might learn to think:

- sometimes I don't focus well, but I am getting better at it
- what helps me, is to move away from my best friend in the classroom
- if I imagine staying on a path and not going off it, I can concentrate for longer.

Without mindfulness, students aren't alerted that their current state is not the only state available to them. When I was working with one student on self-regulation during my home consultancy, she suddenly grabbed her head to stop herself from looking around at my cat. She had become aware of her distraction, whereas before she'd had no consciousness of it.

Exposure to the idea of mindfulness (that you have control about how you interpret a situation) can be a game changer for students. Without awareness of the possibility to adopt a different approach, students are locked into how they are reacting to a situation. If they are not attuned to their own sense of where they are, they will be locked into their current performance. Through skilful mediation, they can be encouraged to improve their ability by making different decisions, practising new skills or behaving differently.

The development of positive and productive mindsets is a metacognitive activity. I referred to this earlier in the image of affect and cognition being two sides of the same coin. The difference between reaction and reflection can be the difference between stuck on one plane, or stepping onto an upward spiral of self-actualisation and achievement.

How we respond to children's behaviour influences their beliefs about themselves. I was fortunate to learn one of the greatest lessons of my life one day from a colleague in the playground. A child had a broom, and he was just about to whack someone with it.

Think about what you would have done.

My remarkable colleague swooped in and said: 'You are just the person I need right now. You have the broom. I have some sand I need cleaned up this minute. You're strong enough to be one of my best helpers'.

The genius of what she did was to use the words 'one of'. It meant that not only this child, but any child in her hearing, had a new idea of who and what they could be. The broom became quite popular that week!

Formulating the principle that has them articulate the dimension they want to work on is a step towards making students reflective. They understand they have a range of choices, rather than being simply reactive where the choices are invisible to them. Mindfulness is conceptual. For the most sound information, it is best to go to the work of Carol Dweck herself (Dweck 2006).

Formulating a principle is an important step in the application of learning process. Once the principle is packaged, the student is asked to think about where else they can use it. They are encouraged to suggest another place in the curriculum, at home and possibly on the sports field. They are often asked how their parents or siblings might use it, to get the idea that it applies to others as well. This way, transfer becomes an expected part of the learning process.

As educators, we are always seeking to develop students' capacity for three kinds of transfer: content, thinking processes and the positive intellectual attitudes or dispositions they attach to their thinking and learning.

Ron Ritchhart, research associate from *Project Zero*, Harvard, indicates that the 'best and perhaps ultimate thinking-infused program is a curriculum focused on understanding'. He quotes Jerome Bruner (Bruner 1973) to define understanding: 'the ability to go beyond the information given, to use our skills and knowledge in novel circumstances and in the creation of new ideas'.

IN SUMMARY:

- transfer of knowledge and skills is important for transforming knowledge and adapting to change
- transferred knowledge can be flexed for innovation
- planning for transfer increases the likelihood that it will occur
- transfer occurs as near transfer, similar in kind and context; or far transfer, where the context is dissimilar and removed
- the capacity to enact transfer benefits from learning to relate entities to others that are similar and proximal first, before moving to entities that are dissimilar
- three kinds of transfer have been highlighted in this chapter: content, process and dispositional
- deriving universal principles from specific events facilitates the packaging or information for easier transfer.

CHAPTER 6

Avert the Assessment Avalanche

*The best way to find out what we really need
is to get rid of what we don't.*
Marie Kondo

You arrive at work on a Monday morning refreshed and ready to go. You've spent time with your family, contacted a few friends, had a leisurely breakfast on Sunday and went to bed early after reading a chapter of your fabulous new book.

Said no teacher ever.

Dashing to school, bleary-eyed, trailing stuff, wondering how you're going to catch up on last week let alone manage the new one. You tried to have time with your family, skipped over contacting friends, sent the kids to the park with somebody on Sunday (if you have kids, or a somebody) and spent the afternoon doing learning stories, portfolios, observations, checklists, updating the parent book, refreshing the new digital portal with a quick story and some photos and 'Oh no not again!'... writing reports.

(Forgive me if I have made any assumptions about your lifestyle. I do know that there are many different kinds of families in the world.) But it is a metaphor for your relationship with your work. Of all the questions I get asked, 70% are about assessment and reporting.

Assessment, evaluation and reflection allow us to think critically and constructively about our work. They are all part of the process that helps us to monitor and judge the success of the learning processes and how well students have internalised the information. It is the basis of all reporting.

Like planning, your assessment links directly to your vision. You've taken the effort to consider many perspectives about early education. You may even have chosen where you work based on your internal belief systems, and your image of children.

What specific knowledge, skills, emotional tone, competence, integration, curiosity, courage, flexibility, collaboration, types of play, would you like to see? What are the precise features and conceptual building blocks of your place?

Assessment is elevated if you are purposeful about what you collect and curate. In this book, I am hoping to attune you to look for conceptual understanding within your curriculum and to record its formation and mobilisation in both closed- and open-ended interactions with peers and materials.

A school or centre might use some of Steven Covey's (Covey 2013) amazing work to develop a mission statement encapsulating and manifesting their vision. Now you've chosen, design your own assessment plan. Don't compare your context to everyone else. Different philosophies use different lenses and you are looking for what makes your context unique as it underpins your student's knowledge, wellbeing and social integration. Knowing what you want is half the battle.

Eight P's for assessment and appraisal

When we appraise something, we don't only assess what there is to observe, but also what might need to be done as next steps. To do this we can employ the usual suspects: why, what, how, who and when. I have itemised eight P's for assessment and appraisal to answer these questions.

1. Purpose
Why are you assessing? What are you looking for?

The very first thing to consider is what is prescribed. Is there a national, federal, state, municipal or school compliance framework, document, process or report that you have to attend to? If there is, make a plan for that first. It might even be outside how you want to report on your preferred process, but accept it. Combine capturing evidence of prescribed outcomes at the same time as you capture what relates to your vision. And as much as possible use the same systems you put in place to accomplish both. Streamlining is the best course of action.

Plan your desired assessment. Usually you're looking for social connection, emotional wellbeing, cognitive involvement, physical wellbeing, and if it's part of your vision, spiritual wellbeing.

2. Processes

No assessment or evaluation can occur without collecting data. How are you going to do this? You know what you want to collect, so select the processes to do it.

Modern digital modes are extremely adaptable, and online planning, assessment and communication platforms can streamline your efforts because you'll have everything handy in one place. Photography, and video are also useful, but don't underestimate the time and skill needed to organise, edit and keep track of your digital collections. If you do use a digital platform, train everyone to use it and dispense with hard copies of everything. Ensure that the technical support is available for digital processes to avoid time wasting and frustration.

There are many ways of recording data and you should choose three or four ways that all give you different information. There are complex processes like the pedagogical documentation associated with the Reggio Emilia philosophy, but your method should fit your vision and you have to be committed to it. If you are using it, you will research the techniques and eliminate any other kinds of assessment that don't belong in the process.

You can use learning stories, keep portfolios, use short anecdotal indoor and outdoor observations and develop checklists for either physical skills or cognitive skills.

A huge mistake is to hear about what someone else is doing somewhere else – and rushing to include it. STOP! Either adjust what you are already doing, or if you genuinely think it is a better methodology, then adopt it, *but throw out what it is replacing*. You've all heard that it's the last dump of snow causing the avalanche that breaks the teacher's back!

3. Practicality

What can be expected of staff?

The vision and organisation you've already put in place makes allocating roles much easier.

In my centre, the early morning and group discussions were typed up on a computer by my co-teacher as we conversed with children. Prior to this great innovation, it all used to be written down and I used to type it up later. We used documentation of children's conversations and comments as part of our data collection. And when I was doing the typing up of what every child had contributed, and the sequence of the conversation, it made me think more deeply about their conceptual grasp of the content. Reflection after the fact often reveals new ways of interpreting what you heard in the moment and may suggest further possibilities.

As mentioned earlier, in the preschool setting, we usually have the miracle of two adults in the room. This allows one of us to act as a microscope, spending time with a small group for a purpose we had planned and resourced; and the other, as radar, roving and documenting with photos or notes, directing, supporting, scaffolding, resourcing or observing the whole group.

In both roles, we learnt what to document, and what to leave out. *It is not practical to take down everything and neither is it necessary.* What you look for is the thing that adds to the current state of knowledge or emotional tone in your classroom. Nothing should ever be repeated or doubled up. Capture what has progressed or what can be used to propel things forward.

For outdoors, we used a booklet, with each child's name on a page. If we noticed something we were looking for, or which surprised us, we would quickly date and note it down, usually in dot points, and if there were verbatim quotes from children, we took them down exactly as we heard them. Our children would repeat what they said for us and often even asked us to note down their ideas. These snippets might be done on an iPad and then added to the normal digital storage.

In the classroom, it is useful to record the children's comments about their own artworks and products. If it's not practical to turn their work over and write on the back (e.g. the daffodils are dripping glistening globs of yellow paint) or to tastefully write at the bottom of their drawing, you can attach a note with their comments to the front. Their comments are inroads to their thinking, their own awareness of their skills, and a means to track how they are connecting and elevating their knowledge. It is probably a good place to interject that with all the phenomenal new digital means, like photography, digital voice recording, video and sharing capacity, children are actually capable of capturing, assessing and documenting some of their own process and products.

4. Progress

Never duplicate your data. I have seen observations where a particular child or group of children are described three times a week doing the same thing. 'John, Will and Evan returned to the sandpit today. They shared the dump truck they love and used it to build a sandhill.' If that returning is happening day after day, ask yourself why. Would you like to see them doing something else? If not, fine, but for your own sanity, don't write it down again. If you do want to see change, plan the means to move them up the spiral. Then document the progress. We want to track what, how and why things are changing. Focus on quality not quantity.

5. Primary and secondary sources

When you collect your data, it is a primary source. I have photos, I have a typed conversation, I have observations from indoors and outdoors, I have several checklists. Once you have the data it can be repurposed for different requirements.

Photographs you collect both indoors and outdoors can be uploaded into a weekly digital group folder. Once there, you spend a bit of time extracting photos from the general upload into children's individual digital folders. There are programs which allow you to just select a photo and tag it to another folder, so you don't have to recopy and use up memory space on your computer. You have a chronological tableau of what happened within the group. You also have a sequence of important documented information for each child.

We are really snap happy these days! If I look at a photo and I think: why was this taken, when did this happen, how did this start, what happened next – I haven't got the story. It's no use just having a finger on the trigger. What sets you apart is following the story. You are a remarkable journalist rather than a tourist. And the story may continue over a few days or even months. Recognising the full story, gives you entry to the process, thinking, learning, encounter, exploration, product, value, resonance or transference you've captured.

The same photo, or sequence of photos, can be used for many alternate functions. They could be used to discuss at a staff meeting. They assist communication in a parent interview. If you have family meetings with the children present, photos can be offered to the student so they can verbalise what they've been doing, what they value and what they have learned. Repurposing data is a life saver. The photographs, like the conversations, are what captures the pathway of children's learning.

6. Products
Capture, curate, communicate.

Products are the way your assessment is displayed or communicated. Flexible primary data can be quickly accessed and customised into different products. If it's for you own planning, you can have it static on your desktop to review when you need it. If it's to prompt discussion with your colleagues, make a quick PowerPoint. Select and print what you need for a parent reflection book outside the room. Load a photo montage on a digital photo frame. Add it to the collection of documentation you are organising to show the authorities who may drop in unexpectedly, or by appointment, to assess your centre.

What you capture is evidence of your good practice. Send a short description and photo to a specialist working with a child on an issue. Report on the children's progress with them, or with their parents. Share at conferences, in network meetings, in the broader community the great work you are doing. Create documentation panels for your classroom, which interpret and communicate the learning in your program. Convene a school or public exhibition. The same primary data can be reorganised, re-interpreted, curated and presented to accomplish whatever you need. You can copy, paste and customise because you know the deep meaning and value of what you have captured.

7. Private
Private assessments are shared with parents or possibly specialist clinicians working with individual children. They are protected by privacy legislation and are not to be shared with any other parties. This record of a child's personal progress in all domains is usually shared in interviews with parents and your semester and year end reports.

8. Public
The children's curricular progress and play experiences are often presented in a reflection journal, or digital journal for parents to view. This is public data and care needs to be taken that it is fair to all concerned. It is a vehicle for educators to demonstrate the learning journey of children and to make their thinking visible. When it's public, make sure all children are in the reflections at some stage. If parents know that your mini projects are run with small groups, and not all the children are interested in some of them, they'll accept that. But they will expect you to include their child in another mini project sometime in the year. Also be completely aware of the filters we spoke about earlier related to culture, gender and other considerations.

IN SUMMARY:

Regarding assessment, we consider the eight P's: purpose, processes, practicality, progress, primary and secondary uses, products, privacy and publicity.

CHAPTER 7

In Words We Meet the World – Harnessing the Structure of Language

Consciousness is reflected in the word like the sun is reflected in a droplet of water. The word is a microcosm of consciousness, related to consciousness like a living cell is related to an organism, like an atom is related to the cosmos. The meaningful word is a microcosm of human consciousness.
Lev Vygotsky
(Rieber, et al., 1987, p. 285)

Top-level structures

A few times now I have shared moments where a new insight has changed the way I think. One such transformation occurred during a presentation by Brendan Bartlett (Bartlett 2003) in 2013 at a Mind Brain conference in Melbourne.

He lectured on top-level structures of language. The gist of it is, if you understand the structure, you are more likely to understand the content. This is so common sense, it beggars belief that I found it so illuminating. But it's true of everything. If you can't see the structure, then you have an episodic grasp of it. It is just a cog in something, and you don't know what that something is.

This aha moment took my knowledge about the structures of language to another level, where I could mobilise it every minute of every day when I was in contact with children.

The most common cause of overwhelm in any education setting is the lack of time. We just don't have enough! I often hear: 'I'd love to include x in my curriculum, but it is already crammed to capacity and overflowing!'

This chapter is about magnifying literacy, without adding one more second of time to your schedule. And that was the thing that excited me about what Bartlett had said. I was a walking, talking literacy machine. Every time I opened my mouth, I had the possibility to support the children's construction of language.

Also, the literacy artefacts I brought into the room to resource the program gained a deeper significance. Every picture book I read, represented every picture book the children would encounter in the future. The same with every letter, poem, chapter book and drama piece. I had a code to share with them. We could unpack and interpret any literary structure we shared together at their current level of engagement.

When we discuss the seven learning zones in the coming chapters, the importance of language development is a constant motif, because concepts are built on language comprehension.

In narrative or writing there is the ubiquitous structure of beginning, middle and end – or, there is a juxtaposition between two things being compared. Problem and solution; cause and effect, are recognisable structures. Even the humble list is a language structure.

The greatest literature builds suspense because it breaks these structures. It messes with our predictions of what is next. A great novel makes you work hard to build up a picture by drip feeding you information. You make one logical connection at a time. The puzzle starts to unfold about a character's true persona, or the significance of events on a particular day. Logical relationships are embedded across the whole story. Structure is a coherence of things in logical relationships. In the novel we are made to work seriously hard to solve the mysteries – and we love it!

The author who writes the novel and injects the dramatic irony and suspense, and we who enjoy the book, know the rules.

Even the list, is not random. There is not much in common between milk and a toothbrush, unless they are on your shopping list. Then you identify the relationship.

In one instance, Bartlett was working with children who were not natural or motivated writers. All he offered them was a list. Tell me about snakes. So, they listed ten different things about them. Once the list was on the page, the ideas were sorted according to different logical connections. The snake was an egg first and grew later. It lived in a burrow. It was patterned a certain way for its own protection (camouflage), people were afraid of it, but it was of great cultural importance. From kids who were averse to writing, they created a fluid, logically connected, interesting and meaningful story. They had a key. And within the story they surfaced concepts of time, location, function, significance, perspective and culture. All this from a list!

When we open our mouths, we have the opportunity to share these structures with children. Be it preschool or early primary, we can magically build language.

But we're ahead of ourselves – we've started at the top level!

The literacy iceberg

At a teachers' network meeting a few years ago, presenters, Dr Avis Ridgeway (Monash University) and the then Senior Lecturer at Holmesglen TAFE, Chris Celada, spoke about early literacy. They used the image of an iceberg. The very tip of the iceberg is reading and writing. And these highly complex skills are built on an inordinate number of foundational skills.

To write a single letter of the alphabet accurately onto a page, a child has to have consolidated a conceptual understanding of spatial relationships. What is top, bottom, sideways, left, right, middle, curvy, straight, round, long, short, upside down and right way up. Students must coordinate a perceptual motor plan in their mind before activating the muscular, fine-motor control to create the letter 'a'. Besides this, there is the comprehension that the 'a' is a symbolic representation of a sound made by the voice, that it is part of a word that is part of a sentence …

Then, beyond writing letters, students must understand the meaning of the words, the meaning of different kinds of sentences and how all the elements are used to formulate communicative products.

Composition of the literacy iceberg

Literacy is hugely important – and, it is another great cause of debate in the early years. When do we teach the alphabet, or phonics, or early reading? And how do we teach it? Tons of papers have been written addressing these dilemmas.

There is no definitive answer.

Some children are reading by three years of age, some only get there when they are five or six, or even seven. Usually, they are all reading and writing by eight years of age. In Scandinavia, they don't start with reading and writing until later, while in the UK, children are starting at four.

But you shouldn't throw up your arms because there is no precise answer. There are a multitude of things you *can do* as you work with children throughout the day, so that whenever they are able to read, or work towards their pen licence, they have the knowledge and familiarity with language structures to make their efforts fluid and meaningful.

One of the first things you can implement is to be observant of children's explorations of the environment. They are engaging in literacy in a non-verbal way. In her book, *Thirty Million Words*, Dana Suskind offers three ways of scaffolding children's language learning: tune in, talk more and take turns.

Tune in

Leveraging experiential schemas

We already know that the first understanding children have is experiential, and in the discussion on foundational knowledge I elaborated on schema theory, the laying down of sensory memories. But why is it important to know about schema theory?

Knowing the power of sensory learning gives us a deeper understanding of what might be happening in the mind of either pre-verbal children, or children encountering new information from the environment. We see greater significance in their actions, and behaviours.

In older children we can harness this sensory pathway to understanding by offering children metaphors to explain complex ideas. My sister is a maths teacher and she often suggest a sensory memory for children to imagine complex ideas. When they don't know what concentric is, she might say: imagine a dart board. For an expanding and rising pattern, she suggests the crystals in a chandelier. The knowledge and memory of concrete sensory experience is a powerful vehicle for learning in older students, and it is equally based on schema theory.

I watched a two-year-old child conduct an experiment entirely of her own devising. There were tall, long-leaved plants in the playground, and the leaves were attached to a woody stalk. The plants were double her height. She had hold of the stalk and was gently shaking the leaves at the top and making a sound like 'hurrr, hurrr, hurrr' for each shake.

Suddenly she stopped and looked around. About five metres away, there was another plant the same. She gave her plant a few more shakes, then went to the other plant, took the stalk and mirrored precisely what she had just been doing.

She had ignored every other tree, plant or shrub in the yard and had found one that was exactly the same, and anticipated that it would behave the same in her hands. This is remarkable.

When we notice it, we can interpret the processes of comparison, evaluation, prediction and hypothetical thinking she employed. And we are in position to offer her the language that accompanies what she has been doing. 'Goodness, Ella, you noticed that those plants are exactly the same and they are not even next to each other'.

In a three-year-old room, children were given some of those fabulous decorating cards for when you are researching the colour for your perfect feature wall. They were all shades of green and they were displayed with leaves of different colours to match to the cards. It was a great investigation table.

On a comfortable couch, across the room, a child was reading a book on her own. She put the book down beside her and took off. I thought she'd lost interest. No, she went to the investigation table, took three or four of the cards, went back to her book and tried to match the green colours to images in the book.

Again, this is hypothetical thinking, transferring experiences across space. If we know there is experimentation in their actions, we can facilitate children's understanding, articulation of their exploration and their conclusions with greater clarity.

Shared gaze

During tuning in, the adult respects the focus of the child. It is engagement with what the student is doing. The child is open to hearing about what he or she is attending to. (I think this works with everyone, really.) The young student experiencing this, begins to see him or herself as having a respected role in a social dialogue.

An example of how to leverage sensory schemas could be toddlers and three-year-olds carrying buckets of water over a short distance and pouring the liquid into the sandpit. They are 'understanding' what they are doing via many sensations. The way the water behaves as they move becomes apparent to them. They feel qualities of the water – weight, volume, flow, spills. They feel qualities of the sand – absorption, texture, porousness. As they repeat the activity, they adjust their balance, develop a sense of expectation, and engage in prediction. Although the experiential learning is language free, *it can be enhanced by connecting it to language.*

When the child returns after a few trips, we can remark that they are balancing the bucket better, that they are spilling less water, that they are getting better at the task. We can ask what they expect to see. If they have the language, let them answer, or if not, help them fill in the gaps.

'What is happening to the water? Is it sinking into the sand? Does it happen every time?' Then comment, 'You know what to expect now, don't you – you've seen it happen a few times!'

If pre-verbal, they may not fully understand all the commentary, but they will get the gist, understand that what they are doing is clearly of interest and value. It will make them more self-conscious of the task and begin to develop a functional receptive language in context around the activity.

Providing language within the context of the young student's activity and exploration is more effectual than providing decontextualised language.

> *'Language is a process of free creation; its laws and principles are fixed, but the manner in which the principles of generation are used is free and infinitely varied. Even the interpretation and use of words involves a process of free creation.'*
> **Noam Chomsky**

Expand the goals of your communication

We can provide language for specific reasons.

Your comment or question can relate to the emotional aspect of the task, or to the cognitive component. You refer to how carefully the task is being done, that the young person must be proud of their activity, that it has meaning to others, etc.

Some informational comments might be: 'You have the bright red bucket with the white handle' or 'I think this is the fourth time you have completed this circuit! Four times there and four times back! A lot of fun as you work hard!' and 'Did you use your own bucket when you were on holiday at the beach with Mum and Dad?'.

When this conversation occurs around the activity, the child is learning how words occur in language frames. They construct language componentry from responding to repeated patterns. He or she is now able to connect the experience to the world outside of the self. They meet the world in words.

Talk more

Magnify the impact of your words

In our daily communications we can be aware of the language structures we are sharing.

We can say, 'I'm going to ask you a *question*. Which area would you like to go and play in now?' And we can respond when they tell us, with, 'Thank you for your *answer*. Off you go then'.

Similarly, 'I am about to tell you all something' or 'give you a list of instructions' or 'tell you a story'.

But your minute-by-minute speech can scaffold literacy in other ways. Rather than being non-specific and saying, 'Please pick that up', add some context by saying, 'Please pick up that book and put it on the middle shelf. The place feels really organised when things are where they belong, don't you think?'

Your longer response, without taking up much more time, provides the labels for more than one item, adds some location concepts, and gives an explanation for the action.

What is going on in our minds, and our reasons for saying and doing things is generally invisible to children, so *talking out loud*, gives them entry into our thinking processes and access to our logical connections. It helps children when we vocalise our own thinking. Not only do they learn words for things in context, but they also learn about your cognitive processes. And they learn about temporal and spatial relationships.

Thinking aloud is often called soliloquy and children who are party to what we are thinking are more able to make connections. When you talk aloud, over time children develop theory of mind. They understand that others have thoughts and that those thoughts might be different from their own.

When you talk about something, it helps with connection to relate it to the more general category it comes from. Rather than say, 'That is blue', you might say, 'That is a blue *colour*', or, 'That is a square, triangular or round *shape*'. 'Would you like the big *size*, or the small *size*?'

Another valuable hack is to add the process words for cognition. 'I was *planning* for us to go outdoors now, but I *noticed* it is raining. I had to *reconsider* and *change my mind*. I *think* it will be better if we eat our lunch first and *make a new plan* later. Who *agrees* with me?' This instead of either changing the plan without saying anything at all, or saying, 'It's raining, so we'll eat now and go out later'.

We can extend children's short-term memory and comprehension by adding cognitive load. Begin with one instruction and then add one more at a time ensuring that they are still successful at carrying them out. When you frame the instructions, include conceptual information.

'Please put your Lego building where we usually do on the shelf outside to the right of the door.'

'Collect your hat and your lunch from your locker, then cross the foyer, and sit down outside on the top step near teacher Jane.'

And finally, now that you have the reasoning, you can add many examples of your own, and get children to use similes.

'This shape reminds me of something. What do you think it is like?' Children might say, 'It looks like the letter L' or 'It looks like a ring'.

This begins to set children up to understand the use of simile and metaphor, which is so important for understanding figurative and inferential language. When you are talking about something like friendship, caring, or any topic, you might ask, 'What colour do you think friendship is?', 'What's the best shape for friendship?' or 'What is the sound of friendship?'

Setting children up to understand the nuances of language can be done as successfully as understanding the precise meaning of things.

In the last part of this conversation the questions are open-ended. This is key to developing independent and creative thinking. In particular using 'why' questions rather than 'what' questions. Once children have learned from your thinking out loud, these open-ended questions encourage them to think for themselves and provide their own reasons.

'A child who is encouraged to think creatively when very young, will likely have a stronger foundation for learning at the beginning of school. Creativity is not talent or skill; rather, it is the tendency toward exploration, discovery and imagination.' (Suskind 2015)

As Dana Suskind says in her book *30 Million Words*, it's not the *quantity*, but the *quality* of the words that counts.

The reason for discussing language in so much detail, is so that we realise that play on its own is not enough. Through mediation of the educators, be they parents or teachers, students can be scaffolded at a very early age to organise their reasoning and thinking into valuable structures.

This lays down the wiring not only for understanding the here and now, but for transcending the moment and building the neural pathways that habituate connection of ideas. Connection is crucial and the pathways for it have to be actively developed.

In every moment of every day in the early years' environment, this knowledge enables us to enhance our own and our students' understanding. We can use these moments, or they can pass us by.

I have spoken about precision and structure; and this wonderful quote sums up the importance of it beautifully:

> *'A man with a scant vocabulary will almost certainly be a weak thinker. The richer and more copious one's vocabulary and the greater one's awareness of fine distinctions and subtle nuances of meaning, the more fertile and precise is likely to be one's thinking. Knowledge of things and knowledge of the words for them grow together. If you do not know the words, you can hardly know the thing.*
> **Henry Hazlitt, Thinking as a Science, 1618**

Of course, human beings and the world are so marvellous and infinite that in some ways, even the most precise language is not adequate to describe their beauty and complexity!

> *'The struggle of literature is in fact a struggle to escape from the confines of language; it stretches out from the utmost limits of what can be said; what stirs literature is the call and attraction of what is not in the dictionary.'*
> **Italo Calvino**

13 key relationships that organise information

I find this list of questions indispensable when teaching, because it prompts me to precisely consider which concept and relationship I wish students to focus on and elaborate.

1. Qualifying: What is it?
2. Analytical: How can it be analysed into whole and parts?
3. Functional: How does it work? What makes it work?
4. Temporal relationship: How is it placed, related or in time?
5. Spatial relationship: How is it placed or related in space?
6. Comparative relationship: How is it equivalent, similar or different?
7. Causal relationship: What is the cause and effect?
8. Dependence: What is dependent on something, and what is independent?
9. Transformational: What has changed? How and why?
10. Quantifying: How can it be measured?
11. Hypothetical: If this happens, what might follow?
12. Ethical: What is our responsibility in relation to it?
13. Imaginative: How might it be?

IN SUMMARY:

- language has top-level structures that give it logical integrity. Lists, cause/effect and problem/solution relationships, comparative juxtaposition and chronological sequences are examples
- language builds through several levels: from experiential schemas, though labelling, to combining words in phrases and sentences. Sentences combine within more complex goal-oriented formats
- knowing the structures enhances rather than impedes creativity
- language is the bridge between the here and now and the abstract realm in which we both encode and decode our understanding of the world
- language is the way we understand ourselves and others
- language is how we learn about how we learn
- language is how we transfer knowledge across contexts
- according to Loris Malaguzzi, languages are expressive, communicative, symbolic, cognitive, ethical, metaphorical, logical, imaginative and relational (Cagliari et al. 2016).

PART C

The Body – Calibrate Your Coordinates on the Agility Wheel

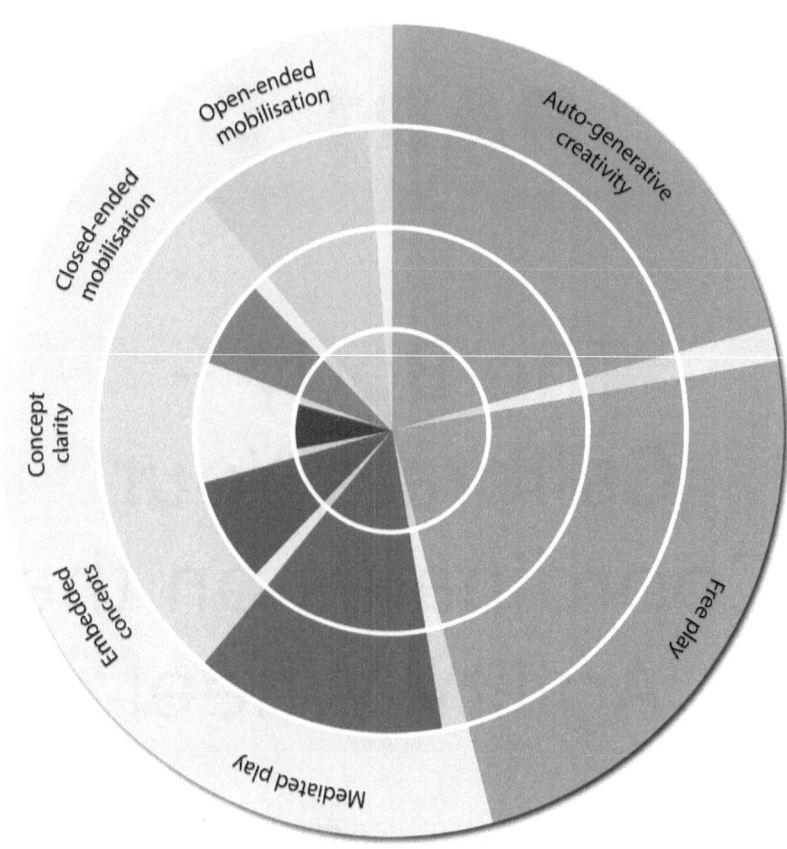

Figure 14: The Agility Wheel

Agility: the quality or state of being agile: nimbleness, dexterity.

CHAPTER 8

The Agility Wheel

No tool is omnicompetent. There is no such thing as a master key that will unlock all doors.
Arnold Toynbee, A Study of History

Agility within and of itself is a strategy.
Pearl Zhu

The ability to think and understand quickly

Pearl Zhu, author and digital expert, describes agility as people-centric, empathetic and focused on improvement. Agile is a state of mind (Zhu 2016). It is not about totally free thinking, but taking account of structure, having discipline and deploying the right skills at the right time.

You spend time resourcing your learning spaces with materials, you plan activities and experiences, you take students on excursions and you organise incursions. All of this is to create a rich and varied platform for learning. Within this planning and resourcing, I am sure you are conscious of wanting to honour the agency of your students, while at the same time, ensuring your curriculum goals are being met.

Previously, I've described you as a choreographer. Now see yourself as conductor.

You can conduct a concerto, where all the elements are known and are practised and performed to perfection. And sometimes that is exactly what you want to do. But at other times you spice up the program with jazz, where the rhythms are set and perhaps even the melody, but the script is open to improvisation, inclusion of new elements, virtuoso performances and creativity. You might even jazz up the concerto!

On the one side of the agency spectrum, an educator controls highly scripted learning and on the other the students have a wide range of choice. The choice can relate to the expanse of physical space, the range of materials, collaborative grouping or the allocation of time to a task. Between very close scripting for students and students' free range, there are many other configurations. But in essence, as the agency of the educator and student shift, the dynamics and the relationships shift too.

The shift involves changes in the role of the educator and the role of the student. As learning becomes more scripted, the teacher moves in and the range of choice narrows – the learning goal is predetermined and specific. When creativity is the focus, the teacher steps away and the range of choice widens out.

I think it is important at this stage to state, that even when the students' range increases, their activity is usually still part of the overall curriculum vision. Learning zones are about giving students more agency in how the projected learning is encountered and acquired.

There will also be times, when student-initiated investigations or projects are given great value and included in the plan. But when we talk about creativity, we are not randomly following multiple paths. There is intellectual rigour – not randomness – behind the use of the zones. Intellectual rigour that values both conventional closed-ended vertical learning and the creative use of conceptual learning towards open-ended destinations.

In Part C of this book, I invite you to engage with seven learning zones, each with its own distinctive form and character. The rationale for doing this, is to prime you to shift zones and deploy each with the same fluency you use when you are driving your car. You can change gears, change directions, change speed and change the destination to ensure that students' learning is optimised.

In any learning zone, there is a three-way relationship between the educator, the student and the task. The word 'task' here is not the traditional definition of a task set by a teacher, but rather, what is currently being attended to in the brain. The task is the current cognition. So, using a rake to gather leaves in the playground for jumping in to enjoy the crunching sensation, is a task.

When we are direct teaching, there is a close connection between the teacher and the task. The teacher has more control over the task. The student is the receiver of information and instructions.

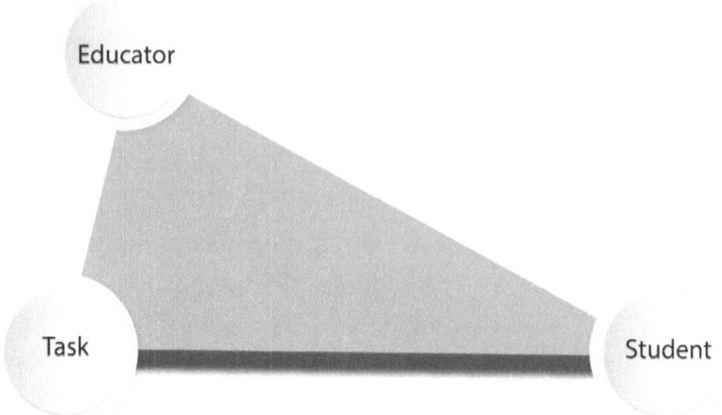

Figure 15: Educational configuration 1

If the agency of the student is magnified, then the zone will change. The task will move away in distance from the educator and the range of choice for the student will open up.

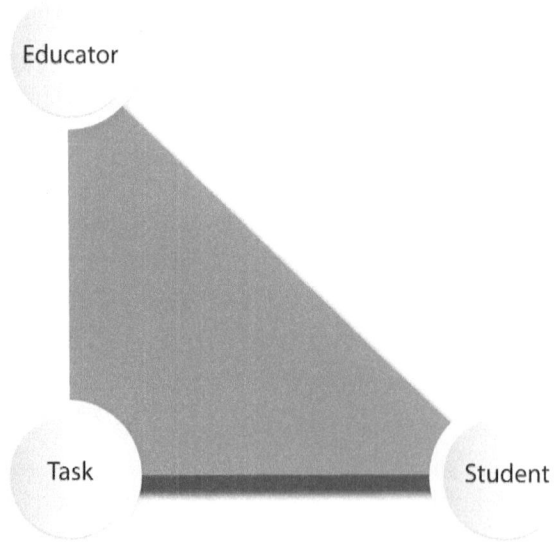

Figure 16: Educational configuration 2

In addition to the change in agency, the education can be one-tiered or two-tiered. The learning can be content-based or include awareness of thinking processes. Understanding the processes and relationships within and across content is what makes the knowledge more transferable. You can teach concepts or amplify the effect and teach for conceptual understanding.

The seven characteristic learning zones are represented on an Agility Wheel. The wheel has four concentric circles, each at intervals of one unit in measurement from the centre. And I have distributed seven zone maps within the 360° area. I have left 5° between each zone to emphasise that they *are independent* of one another. Each zone is defined by two measures: a linear distance representing the proximity of the educator to the student and an angle in degrees, representing the range of choice available to the student.

Starting at a unit of 1, is strategic, because we can never be at 0 proximity. At no stage can we be in the mind of the child. But level one is the closest and most directive we can be. So, for example in free play, the teacher is four units away and the child has 85° of choice (4:85°).

The 7 learning zones:

- Free play (4:85°)
- Mediated play (3:50°)
- Embedded concepts (2:30°)
- Concept clarity (1:25°)
- Closed-ended mobilisation (2:25°)
- Open-ended mobilisation (3:35°)
- Auto-generative creativity (4:75°)

As mentioned above, the range can refer to physical range, where children have more geographic freedom (as in free play) but mostly it relates to the intentional landscape. Being clear on the goals of each of the participants in each zone is key.

Clearly, other educators may like to either expand or reduce the range or distance of a zone, or even add other characteristic zones, but the general idea of the relationship between proximity and range of choice will prevail. The zones I have defined here have been formulated during decades of working with students of all ages. They are common learning configurations in educational contexts, particularly in early years' environments.

At this point it's also essential to note, that the learning zones are *not learning stages*. Each one is independent of the others and they have different goals. They offer the educator the ability to maintain an agile stance. In addition, the size of the segment in the Agility Wheel, does not relate to its importance or to the time it should take up in a curriculum plan. *Every zone is equally valuable.*

The projected use of the wheel is that teachers will be able to easily distinguish the zones. They will be able to balance their curriculum by planning for and resourcing in accordance with the relationships in each zone. They will be able to recognise the opportunities to pivot from one zone to another to leverage a current incident, action or idea. They will have the awareness to use what is happening in one zone to further a goal in another. In short, to have the *agility* to know where and when to animate any one of the zones – and this could be in prior planning or in current process. Educators become hyper aware of the flow of their own and their students' agency.

In the seven chapters that follow, each learning zone will be defined and discussed in terms of its distinctive elements. The roles of the educator and student are outlined, along with suggestions for relevant resources, ideas for scaffolding concept learning, categories of assessment and means of evidence collection.

IN SUMMARY:

- the Agility Wheel represents seven distinctive learning zones
- within these zones, the agency of the teacher and the child change: in some, the student has more freedom to follow their own goals, while in others the range closes and the activities are more scripted by the educator
- each zone is given two measures – the first is related to proximity or distance of teacher in relation to the student and the second refers to the students' range of freedom to select their goals and activities
- the distance is in units 1–4 and the range is measured in degrees
- the zones are independent of each other, not stages in a learning cycle
- the size of the segment for each zone does not represent importance or time spent in that zone; it is about the different interactions, roles, and goals of the student and educator
- no segment has a specific relationship to the segments adjacent to it
- the educator may plan a zone and deploy it for curriculum purposes; but he or she may pivot into another zone to optimise a current, incidental situation
- the ranges selected are based on the author's experience over decades of teaching with different year levels including a lengthy time in early years education. (How long will not be disclosed!)

CHAPTER 9

Learning Zone 1 – Free Play

The playing adult steps sideward into another reality; the playing child advances forward to new stages of mastery.
Erik H. Erikson

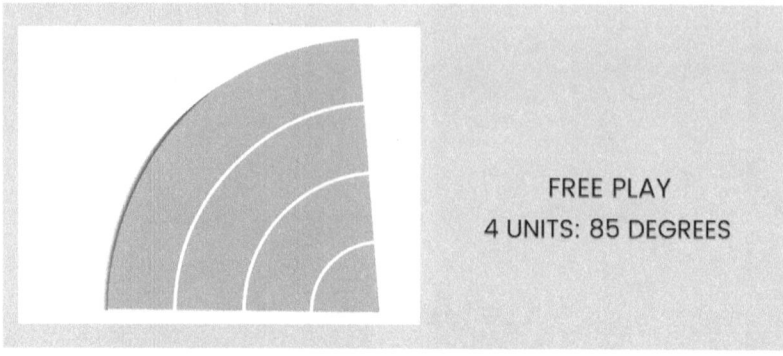

Figure 17: Free play

Coordinates

Students' free play occurs at the maximum distance of four units from the educator on the Agility Wheel, and students have the widest range of choice at 85° (4:85°).

Definition

Free play is a learning zone outdoors or indoors in which children follow their own lead. They select the equipment, materials, location and playing partners to suit an activity of their own devising. They formulate their own goals and are often in a state of flow. It is the least scripted learning zone. Whatever they are learning is self-initiated.

The educator's role involves:

- selecting and providing a broad array of equipment and materials for children to use independently. Some standard materials are always available, and for novelty and variety, others are introduced for short periods of time
- providing materials and equipment to support the enhancement of physical and cognitive skills

- considering equipment to encourage individual and collaborative play
- being prepared to move into a closer range with children who wish to engage with an adult
- observing and assessing social and emotional patterns of behaviour and wellbeing
- interpreting what children might be thinking and learning as they explore the environment.

The students' role involves:

- choosing their own play companions
- practising and consolidating social and communication skills
- exercising independence and selecting from an array of equipment and materials
- being fully immersed in their own world following personal intentions at a self-defined pace
- internalising the qualities of materials and how they transform in relation to different influences in the environment
- developing language competence, sense of self and theory of mind in the company of their peers.

About free play

Seriously, a chapter in a book cannot for one second capture the meaning and value of play! You know it and I know it. There are some excellent books on play-based learning with an enormous body of evidence about its importance for learning (Walker & Bass 2015), (Singer, Golinkoff & Hirsh-Pasek 2006).

There are several well documented kinds of play. Children engage in individual play, parallel play, interactive play, fantasy play, tabletop play, physical movement and games, digital, virtual and other kinds.

Play is good for social and emotional wellbeing and education, as well as cognitive education. The range of resources for children to utilise is endless.

Figure 18: Child absorbed in play

Sensory learning is extremely relevant during free play. You will remember the examples of children carrying water, shaking plants, and other means of understanding the world through their senses. Because of your awareness of this pathway to learning, I am sure that as you observe play, you will be attuned to sensory learning and interpret what might be going on in children's thinking as they manipulate and use materials and interact with one another.

Figure 19: Free water play in group

Your assessment when children are at play, is generally done at a distance. In the preschool, no play goes unsupervised. So, you are in a situation where you can map and observe patterns in children's play without scripting it or getting involved. You notice whether children are constant loners. If solo play is out of character for their peers, you can consider the reasons, and if you need to do something to change the current situation, you can plan it. If children always have the same group of friends, you ask yourself, is it worthwhile implementing strategies to introduce some flexibility? Are children only using one or two areas and not being very adventurous?

At one of the schools where I consulted, the educators mapped the geography of children's play in the outdoor area each day. Over time they noticed that children gravitated to naturally vegetated, more private and shadier areas. They also noticed which materials and equipment were more popular, which caused the most conflict and what introduced harmonious play. They fully took on board the idea of listening to the children and respecting the image of the child (Rinaldi 2001). They used the free play zone as an opportunity for research to elevate their practice.

When children are in unscripted play, it doesn't mean that they won't seek out the educators. But they choose the distance. If you want them to engage with you, you need to be approachable and open. From free play, more scripted activities can develop when children share their thoughts. I discussed earlier the wings project which started this way.

If there are difficulties or conflicts, they will generally surface. When you deal with these situations, in effect, you have shifted zones. You move closer to listen, to arbitrate and educate for fairer or more harmonious outcomes.

Free play is also a place where you can observe the development of children's gross and or fine motor coordination. When I was working with a child who was left behind in the pre-skills for reading and writing in prep, it was clear that many of the milestones for gross-motor and fine-motor skills were unpractised and unconsolidated. Right and left-handedness, crossing the midline, perceptual motor planning and coordination are all important for reading and writing. You can keep checklists and observe children, or have a fun event, where everyone hops, skips, jumps and gallops across the basketball court one day, so you can ensure everyone is progressing well.

Over time, you check that they can roll, balance, run, hop, skip, gallop, jump, slide, climb, hang and alternate movements fluently. You can also check gait, stance, posture and rhythm. Gross-motor development precedes fine-motor development, so during free art activities and table-top play, you can also notice if children can pinch, clasp, lift, cut, paste, carry objects, arrange materials, hold and use painting, drawing and writing implements, roll (e.g. plasticine and clay), stack objects and balance objects.

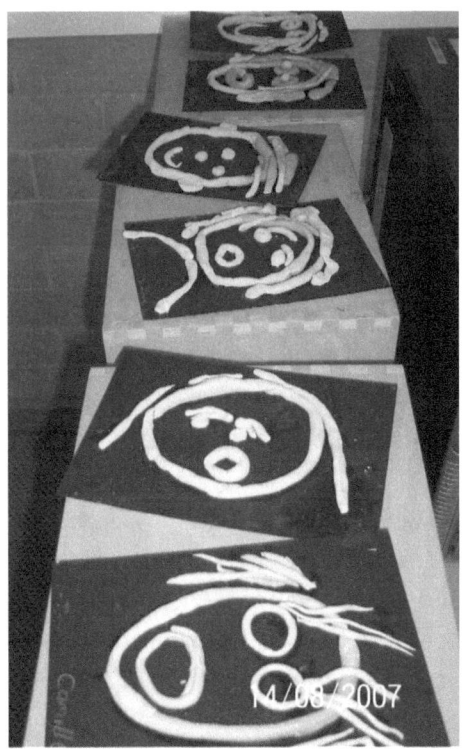

Figure 20: Rolling and pinching techniques for clay

I think it is important to attune the early primary educators among you to the cognitive and conceptual, rather than the wellbeing and emotional, advantages which can be gained through play. Many of you already know its value. But curriculum demands, or parent expectations, often drive play out at the primary level. Independent play can be the basis of great learning and creativity. This is especially true for literacy and mathematics education.

In several of the schools where I have consulted, primary teachers were sceptical about the curricular value of play. But they were prepared to experiment, and they timetabled a play session every morning while parents were dropping off their kids, and for about 20 minutes after that. They were immediately aware of how it revealed students' knowledge, interests and motivation to learn.

When the group assembled for the day, the children, either on their own or with their play companions, communicated to the whole class what they had been doing. The teachers were staggered by the complex interrelationships within the play, the quality of the use of materials and how the play was often infused with what children were learning in other areas of the curriculum. Children from foundation though year two were documenting and elaborating their own ideas and products using voice recording, photography and other applications. When the teachers compared standard literacy and maths statistics with those of students in prior years, they were amazed at the increase overall in the measures for both maths and literacy skills.

Children's play is highly complex. It displays principles of order, use of prior knowledge, creativity, hierarchical relationships, communication, negotiation and total engagement. Free access to construction, art, literacy or science-based activity engages the senses, the mind and the emotions to cohere in the formulation of skills and understanding.

During free play your role is that of an observer, assessor and researcher rather than an active participant in learning goals.

IN SUMMARY:

- during free play, the educator is at a unit of four in distance and the students have the widest range of choice at 85° (4:85°)
- free play is extremely important in early years' settings
- its relevance and value in emotional, social and cognitive development is well documented
- when assessing play, we gain from mapping the way children interact with others
- we can plan to improve children's social and emotional wellbeing by being alert to the patterns of their emotional tone and integration
- it is valuable to map both children's negotiation of play, including where they spend most their time and what they are employing in their play
- there are endless resources for play, and it is an activity that motivates children to discover and explore
- play is as important in primary settings as in preschool settings, but children engage with concepts at a more complex and abstract level
- students are at liberty to approach educators during unscripted play, so it is worthwhile to remain open to their willingness to engage
- from free engagements with educators, new projects might ensue, or children's thoughts can be included in the learning flow elsewhere in the program.

CHAPTER 10

Learning Zone 2 – Mediated Play

... to understand something is to assimilate it into an appropriate schema.
Richard Skemp

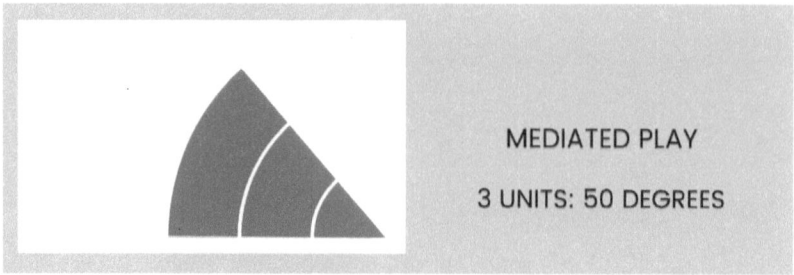

Figure 21: Mediated play

Coordinates

During mediated play, the educator is proximally closer than in free play at a distance of three units. The students' range of choice is narrower, but still fairly extensive at 50° (3:50°).

Definition

Mediated play is a learning zone outdoors or indoors in which the educator steps into students' play to elicit concept learning. The equipment provided is more restricted than in free play. It is selected for its potential to demonstrate learning concepts. Students still formulate their own goals and intentions. The teacher enters the play, not to direct it, but to extend it in the direction of the students' own goals. Before offering information or equipment, the educator listens to the children's own ideas and elicits their explanations. If needed, the educator provides vocabulary, introduces concepts or offers explanations relative to what the children are already doing. The students' play is not scripted, but the educator's mediation is intentional and purposeful. The goal of mediated play is to enrich the child's own play with relevant contextual information about their own activity and thinking processes. Mediated play is a version of shared gaze, where the educator joins in what the children are already doing.

The educator identifies opportunities to assess receptive language, enhance vocabulary and expressive language, to improve skills and to broaden conceptual and relational understanding using scaffolding techniques. They are also listening for ways to extend ideas children have imagined or created as impetus for further learning.

During mediated play, the educator facilitates students' growing conceptual understanding of a variety of concepts over time. There is no immediate time frame for full comprehension.

The educator's role involves:

- assessing the students' current understanding of selected concepts
- considering the next level up in students' conceptual understanding
- where appropriate, suggesting extensions for the play
- respecting the goals and current activity of the students and 'sharing their gaze'
- selecting and providing an array of equipment and materials for children to use independently, which are chosen for their potential to demonstrate concepts
- purposefully and intentionally stepping into children's play as a mediator to enhance and progress conceptual knowledge and understanding in the direction of the student's own intentions
- observing and assessing what children are doing to provide novel vocabulary, bring awareness to concepts and provide explanations if required.

The students' role involves:

- choosing their own play companions
- practising and consolidating social and communication skills
- exercising independence and selecting from the available materials and equipment

- being fully immersed in their own play following personal intentions at a self-defined pace
- responding to alerts from the educator to new language and concepts related to their own activity
- internalising the qualities of materials and how they transform in relation to different influences in the environment
- developing language, concepts and significance of what they are doing in relation to universal knowledge they are working to master over time.

About mediated play

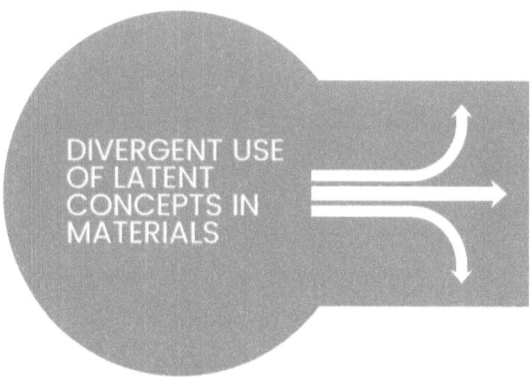

Figure 22: Divergent use of latent concepts

In mediated play, you offer a narrower selection of resources than in free play. Whilst you are aware of the potential of the materials to demonstrate several concepts, *you are not particular about which concepts are activated during mediated play*. The mediational scaffolding is done around students' own intentions. You are focusing where the child's interests lie and expand thinking from there. From the many latent concepts, you choose the one or two directly relevant to the current play.

Figure 23: Big block play

A block has weight, height, width, volume, etc. The idea in mediational scaffolding is not to emphasise all of them. You tune in to what the child is doing with the block, and surface the relevant concept. The child might not need information about the dimensions of the block, because it is being used as a telephone! The concepts to surface then, are around formats of communication. The child has invested the block with an idiosyncratic meaning, and you enter the play respecting that.

As the child talks into the block, you ask: 'Who are you ringing? Did they say hello back? What is the message? Are you making an appointment?' The object represents the format of a conversation, with its purpose and reciprocal structure. Talking on the telephone relies on vocal communication without the additional codes of gesture or facial expression. (Unless of course the kid is pretending to be on FaceTime!)

Direct learning versus mediated learning during play

When a student encounters and uses materials, there is direct learning. The materials give direct feedback. The learning may include language, but it might also be solely in the domain of sensory or perceptual motor understanding. I've often stressed that this is not to be underestimated. Sensory intelligence attunes our proprioceptors, so we successfully move and position ourselves and objects in space. It is also vital for motor planning, which is a sub-skill in writing and many other educational tasks. It is only when you work with a child who does not demonstrate automatic perceptual motor acuity, that you realise how important it is. Perception is not only related to the physical world. For instance, it is a motor perceptual skill to mentally connect two dots with a line before you actually draw the line. Without the perceptual plan the physical attempt might fail.

Your goal during mediated learning is to move children beyond direct sensory or motor learning to enhance and progress conceptual and relational understanding.

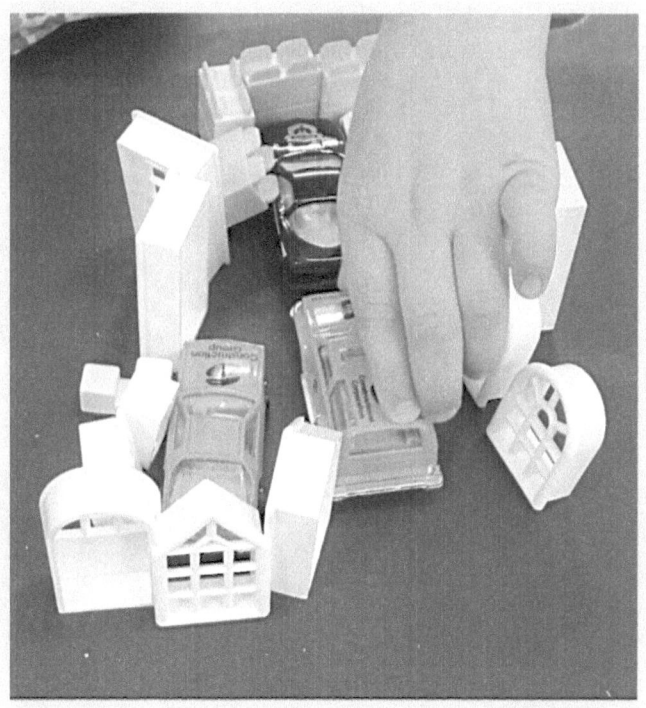

Figure 24: A child sensing enclosed space

The idea is to link children's current activity and exploration to world knowledge. You want them to identify their explorations with new nouns and verbs. To use vocabulary to explain relationships, so that they can mobilise the learning in new contexts. Examples of the kinds of concepts you can highlight are colour, form and shape, size, number, measurement, orientation in space, similarity, difference, equivalence, function, texture, time, sequence, order, seriation, grouping, change, causation, pattern and symmetry. When surfacing these concepts, it is not the idea to give definitions of them, but to encourage children to 'wonder' about them. What do they see or think about them?

Figure 25: Comparison and measurement

You don't use all these words, only what is appropriate. When children are carrying something heavy, you can ask them if it is more or less heavy than something else. (Comparison.) You can ask them why they think it is very heavy. (Causation.) Ask them to explain where objects are in space, like what is at the very top, the first, last or middle thing. (Location.)

When kids are lining something up by colour, you can talk about matching, sorting or grouping. When they use material to build a dinosaur lair or a bird's nest, we can alert them or extend their knowledge to habitats or life cycles.

You observe what they are doing and inquire into their actions or the narratives they are weaving. Their actions and descriptions reveal their levels of knowledge, their interests, and the progress in their thinking over time. This is active assessment.

There is no doubt that what occurs in mediational interactions can be leveraged to further curriculum goals. The interludes and conversations can be brought to the attention of the whole group. The child or children who were the protagonists explain their ideas and discoveries and the *ownership is attributed to them.*

Collecting evidence

Besides the cognitive goals, this is also an opportunity to observe children's perseverance, frustration levels, blocking, cooperation, collaboration and other dispositional and affective aspects that affect learning.

Evidence of learning is collected using photography or video, recording brief conversations, taking quick observations, using lists to tick off on consolidated skills. And as discussed earlier, be aware of capturing the whole story. Sometimes this emerges over a few days or even weeks, rather than in a single play session.

The assessment can be done for early maths, literacy, fine-motor skills, construction, logical reasoning, planning, extension of previous efforts and many other areas. For early maths you might be assessing number, sorting, shape recognition, patterning, symmetry, spatial awareness, one to one correspondence and base 10 concepts.

Scaffolding and extension

A mediational intervention is often the small prompt a child needs to connect with their own motivation and to switch on vistas of knowledge. Drawing is a good example of this. Some children have a natural ability to look at an object, extract the salient features and set to work drawing it. Say it is an elephant. The drawing may just be a curly line and an enclosed shape, but the information has been transposed.

Other children find it difficult to separate the individual elements from the gestalt. They benefit from being asked mediational questions like: What is this animal? What parts do you see? Which is the front, and which is the back? How many legs does it have? Is the tail thick or thin? What shape is the body, head, ears, etc. Which part would you like to draw first?

During these mediational question, the student's attention is directed to how the whole and parts are related and to the features of each part. When the child has gone through the different parts, they are more likely to see a way to transpose the elephant into drawing. Once the process is repeated a few times, they carry it over to other situations. A particular student who joined my K4 group late one year, needed only one such interlude. In the first mediated drawing experience, she drew a butterfly using two shapes, an oval and a triangle. She moved from being completely blocked to being one of the most proficient drawers in the group. It switched her brain on to the technique. Suddenly she could *see* to draw.

A second example of unlocking awareness was with a child who was dependent on a particular play partner (his cousin) and play area, (Lego building). His choices were Lego build with cousin, or Lego build on your own.

On one occasion, he and his cousin had been away for a camping weekend. Trying to shift the dependent child's repertoire, I asked them to draw their experience together. When they brought it over after a while, I suggested they take some blue paper to represent the ocean.

They enthusiastically went to the paper shelf for the paper and collaged an ocean. They returned, hesitantly, and asked if they could use different colours of paper for other things. I said, 'Sure, use what you need.'

Eventually the drawing was swamped under collaged paper and the project had morphed into something, well ... experimental.

During that one experience, the child described as dependent, had the realisation that the room was full of resources. And that they were at his disposal. They had always been there, but he had not been *switched on* to them. From then on, he moved freely around the room and was happy to join in play with different children if they were using anything he found interesting. He gained mastery over materials.

When this kind of learning takes hold, it transforms a mental structure. From the 'I cannot' it becomes 'this is how to do it'. Vygotsky describes how through learning, cognitive structures can rearrange themselves and the transformation is enduring (Vygotsky 1986).

Collecting evidence

Your observations, conversations and interventions will turn up evidence of learning related to embedded concepts. How do children name and label what they are observing? How do they describe their activity with the materials; or explain any relationships or transformations they observe? How do they manipulate, use and give meaning to what they are doing?

You can determine whether to accept their interpretations and explanations verbatim at this point. Their words and actions will uncover levels of knowledge and thinking. Often in their explanations of phenomena, children give the materials human qualities, a process called anthropomorphism. They will say that a shadow moved away because it wanted to hide, or that the magnet has a piece of magic in it. It is up to you where you draw the line towards more conventional knowledge. These early logical connections are often where the most interesting possibilities for imaginative learning reside.

If you decide to introduce new, conventional terms for the concepts and the effects of the interaction of materials, notice how easily they are taken up and articulated by the children. How keen are they to share their discoveries with their peers or with their family?

Scaffolding during mediated play experiences

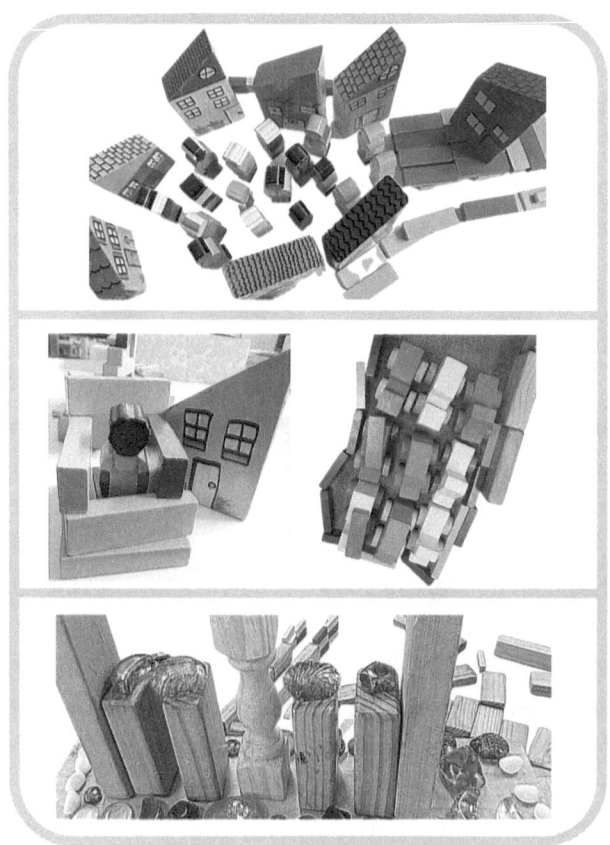

Figure 26: Small block play

Here are some sample scaffolding goals and interventions (this kind of questioning is important in other zones too). These questions can be asked of an individual child, or a group if the play is collaborative.

Learning Goal	Sample intervention
Enquire into child's current knowledge and ability to express their actions	I'm really interested in what you're doing, can you tell me about it?
To provide labels the child does not know yet	What I see you doing here is putting things that are the same together. This is called sorting. You've sorted the blue, yellow and red shapes into groups that belong together. You are sorting by colour. Can you sort by shape? What would you have to do?
Expand the activity to a new level of thinking	I notice that you have enclosed all the sea animals together and all the land animals together, they each have their own habitat where they are most comfortable. I wonder where insects like to live?
Highlight thinking and metacognition	I can see you are solving a problem about how to balance your building. You've tried two different ways, which is the best?
Extend logical and creative thinking	This car you've drawn has great details. Where is it travelling to? Can you add that to your drawing?

Extend commitment and focus	The flowers you've painted are so colourful. There is space to add other parts of the flower. What else do flowers have? Do you have time to add some more details?
Provide an opportunity to change the modality	The student might be offered the opportunity to draw their block building, or construct something based on a drawing. They might be asked to create symbols for sounds they are making or narrate their story for you to capture in writing.

Often during mediated play, you come upon examples of exceptional creativity. A child in my group once constructed paper puppets. They were very simple. She drew two faces, each on its own A4 sheet in portrait orientation. Then she folded the paper and used sticky tape on each of the doubled bottom corners to hold the fold in place. She slipped her hands into the fold and moved the paper puppets up and down to animate them.

What is remarkable was her perceptual knowledge of spatial concepts. She had drawn each face in the bottom half of each page, so that when she folded it, the faces were right side up. She also folded the paper so that the faces were on the outside. All this without using trial and error. In effect, she had manipulated all these spatial conversions in her mind prior to commencing drawing. This is a remarkable feat for a four-year-old child.

Margaret Donaldson says:

'There is a distinction to be drawn between trying different actions to achieve a goal and reflecting on these as a possible set of actions before

performing them. This latter activity – the planning kind – involves the temporary suspension of overt action and a turning of attention inwards upon mental acts instead. Developmentally, the course of events is from an awareness of what is without to an awareness of what is within.' (Donaldson, 1984)

Mediated play is a place where we are moving the awareness from without to within.

In many classrooms, projects like these puppets are ignored or missed, because we might not be looking for the conceptual understanding within them. They might not even make it to the fridge door and be discarded in the daily clean up.

IN SUMMARY:

- mediated play has a distance of three and a range of 50° (3:50°)
- a selected range of resources are provided for student's free investigation and exploration
- mediational scaffolding is aimed to enhance children's thinking around their independent activities
- educators engage with students at the intersection of the child's focus and intentions related to materials
- during mediated play, teachers interact with children and provide goal-directed scaffolds to enhance customised conceptual and relational understanding
- the scaffolds relate to elevating language and labels, emphasising thinking processes, crossing modalities, extending attention span, adding details and moving the thinking from here and now to more generalised thinking
- educators are alert to narratives students bring to their play which can be the impetus for further learning and creativity
- evidence is collected through digital means like photography or video, recording conversations, capturing brief observations or using lists to check on consolidation of skills in different domains.

CHAPTER 11

Learning Zone 3 – Embedded Concepts

A hologram is a photographic recording of a light field, rather than of an image formed by a lens, and it is used to display a fully three-dimensional image of the holographed subject. [Wikipedia 2020]

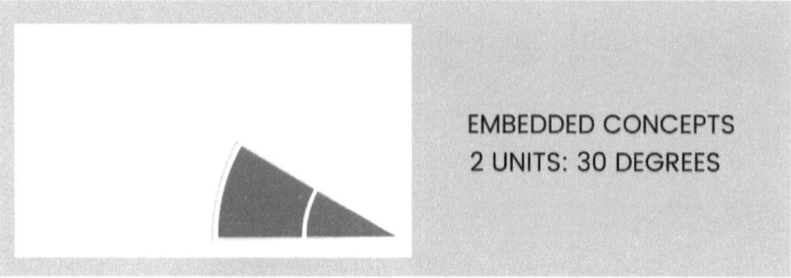

Figure 27: Embedded concepts

Coordinates

In the Agility Wheel for embedded concepts, the educator is at a distance of two units and the students' range is 30° (2:30°). The balance in this configuration is weighted towards the educators' curriculum goals.

Definition

The zone of embedded concepts, whether indoors or outdoors, relates to the educators' intentional provision of resources to fuel and propel specific concept learning outcomes. Embedded concepts reside in objects, art and construction materials, procedures, artefacts like books, or digital products such as videos, photographs and video games. In this zone we highlight what the educator selects and how the resources are deployed to animate selected conceptual learning. Within this zone, the destination is not complete understanding of the target concept, but the provision of relevant investigations that lead students towards concept clarity within a target curriculum area.

The educator's role involves:

- designing learning experiences using resources and materials with embedded potential to investigate specific concepts within a target curriculum area
- arranging the schedule and environment to invite investigation of embedded concepts
- encouraging students to develop, articulate and record their conceptual understanding
- alerting students to the mental processes they are using as they engage with concepts
- assessing, recording and documenting the learning as it emerges for the individual and the group in relation to the curriculum goals.

The students' role involves:

- focusing on a curriculum concept or idea as they use and investigate the selected range of materials and resources provided by the educator
- developing appropriate language to explain and describe the concept embedded in a task
- constructing ideas, acquiring skills and developing processes and procedures related to content
- engaging in experiences and working on products related to their investigation
- understanding concepts through direct manipulation and related discussion, and practising the abstract ability to transfer the information to new contexts.

About embedded concepts

On occasion, during a consultation, I will notice an artful array of materials. When asked why they are there, the educator's answer is often, 'kids just love using them', 'I recently did a workshop on ...', 'I think they add to the aesthetics of the room'...

One such display was a collection of brightly coloured feathers. None of the explanations given, connected the materials to anything else. They weren't connected to ideas like texture, compared to other materials, linked to language or to any particular discipline, even birds! The students' exploration was largely sensory and limited to the feathers.

For learning to be leveraged from our resources, no matter how beautiful they are, we need to be able to answer the question about why they are taking up room in our learning space?

Potential of a pop stick

What do you see when you hold up a popsicle stick, the kind used to bring your delicious ice-cream (my favourite is caramel) to your mouth?

In Reggio Emilia, educators employ the metaphor of a hologram, in which the smallest part of something represents the whole. (Reggio Children 2001).

I love to overlay this idea when thinking about the potential of resources. Every material has latent avenues of inquiry. Before we unlock the ideas of the pop stick, it ought to be noted, that the idea is not to activate *all* the potential, but to *be aware* of potential, and select what will serve the ideas the learning educators have set as a goal. We have already touched on this in mediated play.

The paddle stick starts its life in a white birch forest somewhere in the world, perhaps the US or northern China. The trees are felled, transported through rugged terrains to a distant factory yard where the trunks are stacked and cured. The trunks are cut to appropriate lengths to fit a

Figure 28: Display of materials for teacher workshop

veneer slicing machine. The wooden sections are boiled to make them more amenable to having the bark manually stripped before the logs are fed into a rotary saw to be pared into thin rolls of veneer about 600mm wide. The usual factory has about 40–60 workers. The rolls of veneer are fed through a die cutting machine which prints out the shape of the pop stick. The pop sticks are placed in a drying cavity; and finally, sack-loads are poured into a tumbling polisher, so the end product is smooth and silky to the touch. The sticks have to be packaged, loaded and transported by road, rail or air to the stores where we can order or purchase them.

In this process there is the potential to engage with pop sticks through life sciences, engineering, mathematics, geography, culture, economy. We have not even discussed how the tree seeds, grows, ages, etc. For older students, the potential extends to photosynthesis, transpiration, chlorophyll, changes in expiration from oxygen to carbon dioxide at night, and more.

Apart from the potential prior to the pop stick being in our hands, there is the potential of what we will do with it and how students might use it to fuel their imagination. Sticks can be used to make a photo frame because all have precise dimensions. We can use them for measuring, ruling lines, floating, counting, creating designs, making a mobile ... the possibilities are endless! A quick look on Pinterest will blow your mind.

I think you understand why I said we don't have to enact all the potential.

If you respect the potential of materials, and of all resources, you will give thought to which resources to include in your teaching to achieve your learning goals for students.

Figure 29: Pop stick sculpture

When you select materials for the embedded concepts that suit your planned curriculum, you use the materials in a convergent way. You lead the student from the material to a predetermined destination. (This was the opposite in mediated play, where you selected from divergent concepts to suit the child's intentions.)

Using the latency of embedded concepts is both a science and an art. The science is knowing which concepts can be taught through the use of a resource; and the art is to imagine what they might reveal when children mobilise the knowledge they gain from them.

Embedded concepts are a means to attune students to information *without telling them directly*. It makes the concepts discoverable.

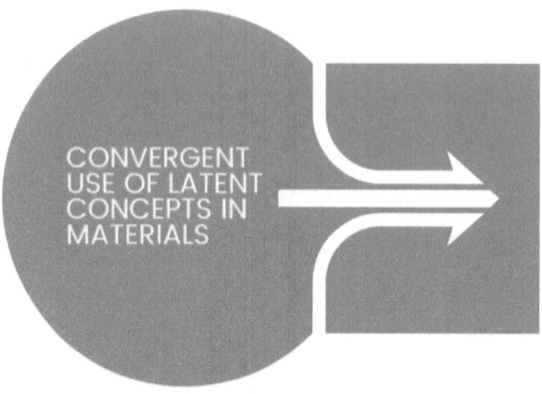

Figure 30: Convergent use of latent concepts

One of the well-researched ideas about efficient flexible learning is that concepts are more easily and permanently understood if they are encountered in a variety of situations (Kilpatrick, Swafford & Bradford 2001). Students gather the data and see what is behaving the same way. What is general or translatable across each of the situations.

Resourcing for embedded concepts

As with any other plan, the goal will drive your selection of resources. And there are two main ways of presenting them: multiple investigation areas eliciting the same concept, or a single investigation area with several choices related to the target concept.

A range of connected experiences across time and space

States of water

The Explorations Project discussed in Chapter 4 went over an entire semester. Water investigation to specifically elicit knowledge of the states of water (solid, liquid and gas) occurred in several different investigation areas over time. Ice was included, so that the melting and refreezing could be investigated.

Figure 31: Exploration of states of water

We used water in the liquid form in a water tray with several jugs, containers, tubes of different diameters and funnels. We provided water on tables with pipettes and eye droppers where children could put drops of water onto different materials. The idea was to introduce the concept of absorbency of materials in relation to whether and how efficiently they might contain water. We asked them to make the smallest piece of water they could.

In a group activity one day, in the safest possible way, water was boiled in an electric frying pan and a cold metal surface was held above the steam for droplets to condense onto. We didn't expect all the children to understand fully the condensation process, but the entire water cycle was embedded in different materials and processes over time.

We put water into balloons, for children to feel the shape of water changing. We provided vessels for pouring from narrow to wide and wide to narrow containers to explore what happened to the volume.

The experiences listed here are skewed to the sciences, however, the arts, cultural narrative, dance and music were also used to explore water. The meanings were not only about water, but our relationship with, reliance on, appreciation of and imagination regarding this miraculous element.

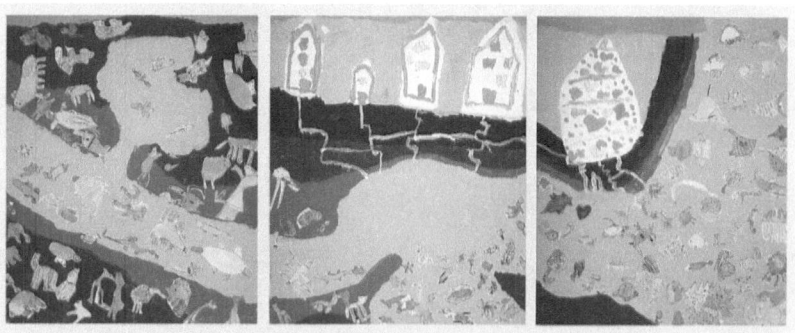

Figure 32: Uses of water triptych

Figure 33: Exploration of Australia's First Peoples' art

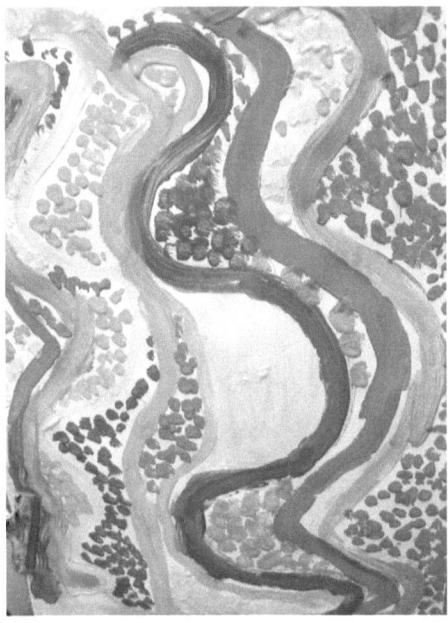

Figure 34: Representation of rainbow serpent

Magenetism

You could do the same by embedding magnetism in several ways across your room or offer students several different encounters with it over time. Most classrooms have metal whiteboards and use magnets every day to secure display materials.

If you are keen for a student to know the different qualities of magnets, such as which materials are attracted to them or that a magnet has two polar opposites, you focus directly on the knowledge you want your students to elicit. You provide a magnet, cardboard and supporting materials. They predict which of the materials will move above the cardboard as the magnet moves below. The students refine their knowledge and understand that the metal objects can be moved, but not wooden, plastic or paper, etc.

To learn about polar opposites, you purposely select N and S bar magnets to develop that knowledge. The intention for the learning is intrinsic to the task. Their investigations have them observe the effect of polarity, to see the forces at work.

This early experience sets students up to later explain the role of magnetism in electricity and how electromagnetism is used as a power source. It will enable them to understand the role of polarity in how solutions move around the human body. One encounter with magnets, or multiple encounters where there is no discussion about what is occurring, will not see them progressively understand this universally applicable force. This extends to understanding the idea that your views about life can be the polar opposite of someone else's.

In embedded learning, students develop a deep understanding of concepts, because the materials are supported by both sensory information and intentional language. They hear terminology in context and the explanation of what they are observing makes sense because they have directly engaged with the materials. They are given time to consolidate new language and advance their curriculum understanding.

Several activities related to a concept in one investigation area

As an alternative to providing experiences across several areas you might set up one area with different materials to elicit the same kind of information. One such example was a light exploration area, where we provided an overhead projector and screen with materials that were selected because they were transparent, translucent, opaque and combinations of those qualities for children to explore. Beside it on a table we also placed a piece of Perspex up about 25cm on blocks with white paper below and provided mini torches. The children shone the torches over a variety of materials on the Perspex that created shadow and reflections on the paper below. They learnt to change the size of the shadows by moving the torch further or closer to the materials. They created complex shadows by using two torches. The information was further mobilised when the children made up a story and created a shadow play. Their knowledge enabled them to control the size of the shadows on the screen.

In this example you see how the potential of embedded concepts is multiplied by lining up several objects so that they act on one another. They can use the relationships between the objects to solve problems or achieve effects. This exploration was captivating to both children's curiosity and imagination and, over time, the experience made them intensely aware of light and shadow, one of the most observable sciences available to us. When learning becomes complex, it is precisely because several things are acting together. So, embedding information in this way, allows the children to experience the effect and begin to unpack the relationships and the role of the different elements in what is happening.

Highlight thinking around embedded concepts

The emphasis is not only on the labelling of the objects and interactions with the materials, but also on the processes of thinking the students use in acquiring the new knowledge.

Teachers lay the foundation for students to use their metacognitive capacity. For example, if you want them to have sound scientific knowledge, you can gradually introduce the methodology of forming hypotheses, observing patterns, recording data, reviewing information and framing questions. These scientific inquiry skills are needed as a foundation for biological, chemical and all other sciences. This is done at the appropriate level.

When you offer an activity with large PVC pipes and things that roll, like marbles, ping pong balls, etc., you can ask:

'What are you going to test out today?'

'Which will roll further, the ping pong ball or the golf ball? How can you measure how far they go? Wow, why do you think that happened!'

'What happens if the pipe is set up more steeply against the sofa? Why do you think so? Will the balls go faster, further?'

'Would you like to draw your experiment to explain it to your friends?'

The materials you provide allow you to surface vocabulary, relationships, thinking and procedures, like the scientific method. You might record when children use words like noticed, explained, remembered, thought that if I did x then y, tried out, learned, compared, thought about, grouped, planned, changed my idea and any other process words discussed in earlier chapters. You can also be alert for theory of mind, where they attribute a thought, idea, plan or change of idea to other children in the group. I often hear children say things like, 'First Daniel thought the heartbeat went slow when you run, then, when we measured, he changed his mind'. This is evidence that children are recognising metacognition in others.

When embedding concepts, we aren't imposing an out-of-context, episodic task and expecting the students to learn and memorise dislocated information. The connections and relationships are clear to them and they are able to transfer the knowledge because they thoroughly understand both the content and the mental processes they used to obtain it.

This chapter has had a significant focus on scientific concepts. But the literacy and art materials you provide can equally surface abstract concepts like friendship, happiness, loyalty, responsibility, power, beauty, imagination or love. These concepts are equally able to be investigated and explored. Stories, poems, letters, puppetry, drama and cultural celebration also contain latent concepts for marvellous investigations. I will leave you to design investigations to elicit these and the one million other concepts you can think of.

IN SUMMARY:

- activating learning through the use of embedded concepts has the teacher at a distance of two units and student applying a 30° range of independent choice (2:30°)
- embedded concepts are deployed when the educator selects specific materials and employs them in a strategic way, so concepts are discoverable by students, not directly taught
- materials, procedures, artifacts, or even excursions and incursions, are selected because they provide inroads to understanding concepts without employing direct teaching
- students benefit from observing, manipulating, and experiencing the concept embedded, either as a single entity, such as a shape, or as something being acted on by other elements in the environment such as heat or temperature on ice, or light on shadows
- embedded materials provide meaningful contexts and experiences to introduce abstract and transferable ideas such as temperature, magnetism, texture or symmetry. It is also a way to introduce through literature and other means, concepts such as trust, friendship, optimism and other abstract ideas
- educators can track and record children's language progress, recognition of thinking processes and metacognitive language, and articulation of different relationships that occur within and amongst different materials.
- the potential of materials and situations to unlock learning is always present.

CHAPTER 12

Learning Zone 4 – Clarity of Concept

Music is powered by ideas. If you don't have clarity of ideas, you're just communicating sheer sound.
Yo-Yo Ma, cellist

Clarity, clarity, surely clarity is the most beautiful thing in the world, A limited, limiting clarity I have not and never did have any motive of poetry But to achieve clarity.
George Oppen, poet

Figure 35: Concept clarity

Coordinates

The clarity of concept learning zone is the closest proximity to students with the most specific educator goals and most restricted choice of activity for students (1:25°).

Definition

The clarity of concept zone is a space where the objective is full comprehension and understanding. It is not a space where we are comfortable if students are moving toward understanding. The zone is not time restricted, so the comprehension does not need to be reached in a day, it can be a process; but the destination is clarity of concept. This is especially important when a base concept is required to support more complex ideas.

The educator's role involves:

- designing learning experiences using processes, resources and materials to ensure a student understands the target concept
- arranging the schedule and environment in order that students learn and mobilise a concept or group of related concepts

- supplying the language and skills necessary to achieve concept clarity
- encouraging students to apply, articulate and record their conceptual understanding
- alerting students to the mental processes they are using as they master concepts
- assessing, recording and documenting the learning as it emerges for the individual and the group in relation to achieving concept clarity.

The students' role involves:

- focusing on and developing comprehensive understanding of a specific curriculum concept or cluster of concepts
- acquiring appropriate language to identify, define, use and communicate target curriculum concepts
- having the ability to deploy knowledge of concepts in application tasks
- generating products that demonstrate and communicate their understanding of the learned concepts.

About clarity of concept

The difference between working on clarity and the three zones I have already discussed, is that we don't want to be working towards conceptual understanding or creating the pathway as before; we want the concept to land. We want to see evidence that a student has the requisite knowledge to move on to something more complex. This is the most prescriptive configuration of the seven zones.

Comprehension of the concept is the prescribed goal, but it does not mean we have to be prescriptive in how the information is presented. We can use the most direct route and tell students what they need to learn, or we can choose a more circular route.

Even in this most proximal zone, we can distinguish between a child learning in a rote fashion which enables them to achieve a task without fully understanding why; and fully understanding why the rote information is valid. Learning the times tables is an example here where simply having the answers immediately to hand saves time, effort and anguish. In many situations using rote knowledge, formulas and rules successfully generates correct answers. They are short cuts. In some cases, this is extremely helpful. But sometimes, without the full understanding there is a ceiling the student will reach beyond which their understanding is inadequate for the complexity of a task.

If possible, it is important for students to genuinely understand the concepts.

The kind of teaching using formulas and rules is called instrumental; and the kind where concepts are understood is called relational. Both are necessary, but they are different.

Reaching clarity through instrumental or relational teaching

Have you ever considered a clock as a number line? If you have, you were many years ahead of me. I was fortunate to attend a maths workshop where the difference was explained between instrumental and relational teaching methods.

Instrumental teaching emphasises procedures and rules and gives the students practice tasks to apply them. Relational teaching aims to uncover the conceptual reasons that underpin the rules (Skemp 1986).

Back to the clock. For the first time ever in this workshop, I mentally opened a circle with numbers on it and converted it to a linear format: a number line from 1–12. It doesn't sound like much, but it was a conceptual revelation to me. I loved the flexibility of a circular number line.

In this workshop, there were other revelatory ideas. In another first for me, I derived the features of a prism for myself. Prior to this, I had misconceptualised a cone as a prism. If you are a consummate mathematician, and you're laughing now, I don't mind. It was so exciting to me that I had *clarified* my thinking.

We want students to achieve clarity – but we can't give it to them. They must construct it. It is common in our educational culture to package information and present it to students using a direct teaching methodology. Sometimes this is exactly what they need, and sometimes it prevents the student from engaging in active thinking and learning around the topic. They focus exactly on what the teacher presents and aren't motivated to explore it or make spontaneous connections between it and other knowledge. They get used to being provided with packaged information. It is like fast food, or processed food for thinking; they sidestep doing slow, integrative thinking. You will hopefully recall here the earlier conversation about how understanding length, ratio and the term 'circumference' are important for understanding pi.

In relational teaching, more emphasis is placed on conceptual and structural information than on rules and procedures. Of course, you need both. But if students can understand the basis of the rules, so much the better. It is good to hold both in mind when we plan activities.

The reason I get so excited about the value of relational teaching is that it can be widely used in the early years because *we have the time* to spend working on concepts in a variety of ways, both indoors and outdoors.

Taking time over new concepts

Proof that you fully understand a concept, is to recognise it operating in diverse contexts. But to get to the stage of recognising and employing concepts in this flexible way, it is necessary to have total clarity about the meaning of the concept in the first place.

Something that often happens when teaching a new piece of information, is that not enough time is spent consolidating it, or too few examples or encounters are provided to illustrate it before moving on.

Earlier, I spoke about selective association, selective discrimination and selective generalisation. In selective generalisation, students can pick concepts and how they work in a very flexible ways – but, they will only do this if they *know what something is*, and what the features are that construct its identity. So first, we must build clarity.

Most knowledge is dependent on other knowledge

Having clarity, is especially vital when knowledge builds in layers or networks. If you don't really understand division, will you understand fractions? If you don't understand fractions, numerators and denominators, what are your chances of understanding variables in fractions in algebra?

Many children move through school from one year to another with gaps in their knowledge. The early years are a time when both vocabulary and structures of language can be successfully taught in engaging informal ways. You can actively introduce knowledge that is the foundation of a conceptual framework for life. So much about knowledge is about measuring things in different ways.

We can scaffold this knowledge in our talking aloud. We can talk about cutting things in half. Having half a piece of paper, changing partners halfway to the playground, reading half the book now and half later. When the students really understand halves, you can ask them to estimate how much water you might need to fill half a container. You are establishing a concept of proportion. Sticking with halves until children really know the concept will make it easier for them to move on to quarters. There are still adults at college who think 1/8 is more than 1/4. Clearly, the idea of proportions and fractions never fully landed for them!

Mary Baratta-Lorton, in her excellent book, *Mathematics Their Way*, advocates giving children multiple ways to solve a particular task or problem. They are encouraged to use illustrations, representations, drawings, diagrams, manipulative materials and small group discussion to solve problems. Block practice and drills can be used, and the repetitive practice can be effective; but drills without comprehension are not durable.

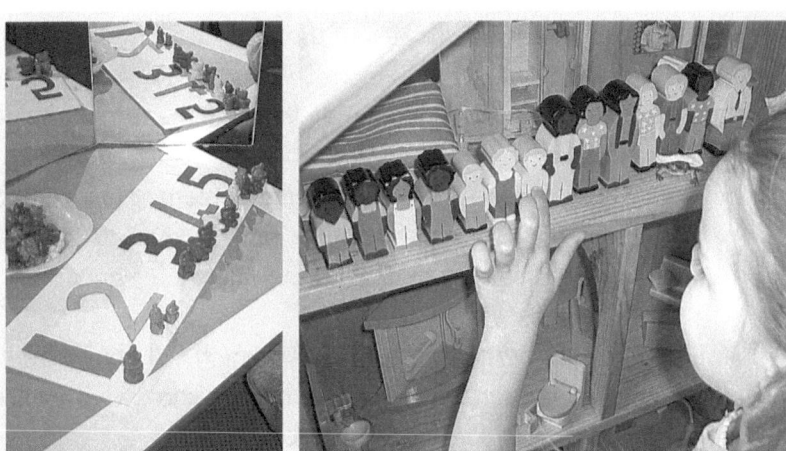

Figure 36: One to one correspondence

According to the Erikson Institute, there are five important concepts that children absolutely need to master to be successful at mathematical thinking over time:

1. **One-to-one correspondence**: In a collection of objects, every object will have a corresponding number
2. **Stable order principle**: You must say the counting words in the same order every time
3. **The cardinal principle:** The last word you say is the total amount (for example, in a group, if you've counted 1, 2, 3, the total number in the group is three). Cardinality is the absolute value of a number.
4. **The abstract principle:** If you have three things in a group, no matter which one you count first, regardless of their colour, shape or size, there are still three in the group. It is the conservation of constancy of number.
5. **Order irrelevance:** It doesn't matter which object in a group you count in which order, you still get the same total.

Children will learn over time that numbers are used in three ways:

- Ordinal number: This relates to the sequence of things, first, second, third, last, etc.
- Cardinal number: As mentioned above, this is the absolute value of the number
- Nominative number: This number names something or identifies it, for example your house number, raffle ticket or telephone number. It has nothing to do with the value of a number.

Neither preschool, nor perhaps certain level primary children, need to know this terminology, but as educators, we need to know what we are working towards for later mathematical success.

I can highly recommend using an online children's dictionary if you need to check on any of your maths facts – the one by Jenny Eather is a great resource (Eather 2020).

Knowledge gaps need to be addressed

At the beginning of teaching a concept (or if students have already investigated topics, ideas and concepts, and they still do not understand them), find ways to consolidate them. Concrete materials, videos, actions, peer teaching or narrative are all avenues that can be used to construct clarity.

One great strategy in the early years is to use the human body as a teaching mechanism. This is a kind of cognition, called 'embodied cognition'. Since time began, we have used our own bodies and our personal perspective to think about and define abstract things (Falikman 2014). For instance, we see the future as *ahead* of us, the past as *behind* us. We say things like on the one *hand*, x, and on the other, y. We talk about having a future *vision*, doing an about *face*, setting a *pace*, having a stiff upper *lip* and making a quantum *leap*.

Drama, outdoor activities and awareness of the body in space, can often be a means to develop understanding of complex abstract ideas. Forming a square, circle or oval shape; standing at equidistant intervals; measuring activities like the number of bunny hops in one minute; or the heartbeat before and after a one-minute sprint – these are all ways to enable students to engage with abstract concepts, but in a way their bodies are involved.

Personal is meaningful (and the basis of general)

When each child's height measurement is graphed on a long paper strip bar graph beside their friend's on the wall in the classroom, there is a good chance that they understand there is a difference in their number and their friend's number. You don't even have to use the term 'bar graph'. The concept is about the difference in the number they counted relates to the concepts of more, equal and less.

Adjust measurements to manageable numbers

You need to calibrate some concepts to the age of the children. When younger children want to measure their height or how long their line of blocks is; don't reach for a ruler with centimetres. Have the children look around the room for something to measure with. Ideally, they will choose something regular, like a pop stick, or a drinking straw. If they don't, you might like to go into the kind of experimentation I mentioned earlier about precision and agreement of measurements.

The longer the measuring tool, the more likely the children are to observe and understand the measuring process. Centimetres may be too fine a measure to begin with and the numbers may be too big for early maths learners. When we measured the children's heartbeats because they wanted to know if they got faster or slower when they went running for a minute, we didn't use the actual heartbeat, but divided it by four or five to get to a number the children could easily understand, record and compare.

The children's ideas, investigations and products can be captured, as discussed before, by recording conversations and using different digital means.

Clarity and emotion

Students very easily come adrift if they don't understand a task. I have mentioned before the inextricable link between cognition and emotion. If there is stress around cognition, it is going to turn up in emotion. You might see a child acting out, being a class clown, withdrawing, blocking, avoiding, being evasive, or even difficult.

As academic Sarah Doenmez writes:

'Learning is about knowledge and skills, but it is also inextricably tied to our perceptions of ourselves. As we face cognitive challenges, we also face challenges to our identity. When we can't quickly resolve these challenges, we are unmoored and drift in a "liquid space". This is the place of liminality. It can be a place of danger or an adventure; it can drown or nourish learning.' (Doenmez 2020).

Knowledge thresholds

New knowledge is always at a threshold. If it is at the upper limit of the child's current knowledge, they might feel confused or anxious. It can be a point where they develop negative emotions about learning, about particular kinds of learning and worse, about themselves. If we sacrifice the student's understanding in the interests of speeding ahead to complete a curriculum goal, we miss the point entirely. From 1911, the words of Sister Jane Erskine Stuart make sense:

'Each mind needs to be met just where it is – with its own mental images, vocabulary, habit of thought and attention, all calling for consideration and adaptation of the subject to their particular case ...' (Stuart 1911)

Sometimes we must go backwards to go forwards. We meet the student where they are and scaffold upwards and outwards from there. To do this, we must know where they are.

Clarity of concept also applies when there is a learning task that you would like all the students to achieve in a specific way. This is often appropriate at the primary level, where children need to have full competence with literacy, maths or other concepts, which form the basis of later, more abstract, tasks. Equally in the early years, self-regulation skills, motor skills and foundation concepts are needed to move on to later schooling. In these situations, we might use, dare I say it, a worksheet (I'm waiting to be struck down by lightning) or an identical task.

Concept clarity needs persistence. It might include verbal telling, repetition and demonstration; but try to use different modalities when working at this stage. Make it hands on and use concrete equipment if necessary. With some students, the educator may need to go back to mediated learning if the task or understanding is outside the child's zone of proximal development (Bodrova & Leong 1996).

IN SUMMARY:

- clarity of concept is a learning zone with the closest proximity of the educator and the narrowest goal selection for students (1:25°)
- the intention in this zone is for the student to completely understand content, a skill or a mental process
- it is preferable for students not to rely on procedures and rules (instrumental learning) without understanding the conceptual and structural principles that underlie the rules (relational learning). Educators benefit from being cognisant of both
- the student should be capable of articulating the knowledge and it should be committed to long-term memory and part of their knowledge repertoire.
- if the student has not internalised the requisite information, steps should be taken to ensure they do. This might mean changing modalities, going back a few steps, creating more encounters or giving it more time.

CHAPTER 13

Learning Zone – Closed-Ended Mobilisation

'Begin with the end in mind' is based on the principle that all things are created twice. There's a mental or first creation, and a physical or second creation to all things.
Steven Covey

Figure 37: Closed-ended mobilisation

Coordinates

Closed-ended mobilsation has the educator at two units and the student's range of choice at 25° (2:25°). There is a sense of equivalence in this zone where both the educator and student work shoulder to shoulder.

Definition

Closed-ended mobilisation of knowledge is when students will activate what they know, to achieve a predictable and predetermined goal. It can go beyond where a single concept, process, idea or symbol is understood, often combining multiple elements to see a task through. Mobilisation is the application, elaboration or deployment of knowledge towards a predetermined destination. 'Closed-ended' is often judged negatively in education analysis. But when we examine the idea, a tremendous amount of what is done in preschool and primary settings, is closed-ended; and it is necessary. We regularly want students to arrive at a specific destination because it means they have internalised the knowledge we want them to have. The emphasis is equally on the process students design and navigate as it is on the outcome. What is limiting, is if we only teach a single path or offer one modality to reach a destination.

The educator's role involves:

- designing learning experiences using processes, resources and materials that allow students to accomplish a predictable or predetermined outcome
- arranging the schedule and environment for problem solving in which students identify and understand the task and sequence the steps towards a solution
- encouraging students to apply, articulate and record their problem-solving strategies and procedures
- alerting students to the mental processes, routines and procedures they are using as they work towards closed-ended goals
- including flexibility and alternative means of reaching a single goal
- assessing, recording and documenting the processes and procedures as they are implemented by the individual and the group to achieve the known goal.

The students' role involves:

- focusing on a task and applying knowledge to solve a problem or reach a predetermined learning goal
- developing appropriate procedures and sequence steps to complete tasks
- using appropriate language to communicate their processes and outcomes
- deploying knowledge of concepts in application tasks towards a predictable outcome
- generating products that demonstrate and communicate their understanding of the learned concepts.

About closed-ended mobilisation

When we teach children to write, at some stage in the process, they must reproduce the letters correctly. At the start of the journey the shape of the letter is given, but students can write shapes in the air, trace them in sand or create them with modelling clay. The destination is letter 'a', but the means to achieving it can be different. (When I talk about writing here, I have in mind the primary setting. In the preschool setting, children can explore pre-writing in many different non-prescriptive ways.)

When we want children to use their number knowledge in maths addition, we set a task. Depending where they are in their learning journey, the task ought to be challenging enough for children to achieve it, but not outside their grasp. As mentioned in earlier chapters, you should always be confident that children have the base knowledge before you extend and introduce something new. Develop the facility with equations, problems and tasks using one concept at a time, to really consolidate them. Before adding a new concept, concentrate on developing flexible thinking around the one you're establishing. If you are doing addition, do it in a variety of different ways before introducing subtraction.

You might be thinking, there is evidence that interleaving (mixing up the kinds of tasks) is better for learning, retention and recall than giving a block of the same kind of exercises. And you are correct! *But* the interleaving should only be done once the children fully understand each of the concepts you'd like to interleave for practising. It is important that children know something well before the interleaving begins. It is a second layer, not an initial practice of concept consolidation (Horvath 2019); (Epstein 2019). The reason the interleaving works after each concept is established, is the spontaneous comparison that takes place as each new task is presented. The student gains fluency with how to adapt their thinking, skill or procedure for each new task in the interleaved sequence.

Closed-ended tasks do not have to be repetitive and boring. Indeed, there is evidence that the more varied and interesting the problems or tasks related to one concept are, the better children internalise the principles (Ben-Hur 2006).

Children love an intriguing problem!

In Chapter 4, I shared the story about a water moving machine, where a child presented the group with an intriguing problem of moving water across the sandpit. In this type of scenario, you may follow-up with more intriguing problems, slightly different in nature and upping the challenge. You don't have to think them all up yourself – loan some ideas from your colleagues! I learned a great activity from one of mine.

One morning, when the students arrived in the classroom, there was a HUGE mess on the floor. ALL the play equipment had been strewn across the carpet.

It was a mega sorting challenge. Everyone was a detective and chose what they were looking for, gathered it and placed it back where it belonged. There was a big discussion about order, role allocation, and how knowing what things were and where they went was helpful. Then it was extrapolated to their visits to the supermarket. Where would they find the ice lollies, and why?

During closed-ended problems, *once children have facility with a concept,* you might introduce reversibility and opposites to test the durability of the knowledge. You might change the perspective and make them the judge! Ask them to select from several products and evaluate them in relation to what they know. Set challenges such as:

- 'You have spent ages learning how to write an excellent sentence. Now I want you to write one that is really bad, then swap it

with a friend and try to make each other's excellent again. Get together and explain what you have done and why.'
- 'You have done this challenging sum: 23 + 16 = 37. (Just checking if you are asleep!) 23 + 16 = 39. Can you make seven addition sums that make 39? Can you make a subtraction sum with the answer 39?'
- 'You have learned now that mixing yellow and red makes orange. How can you create an instruction for your friend to mix exactly the same orange colour as you?'
- 'If I asked you to make six shades of orange, how could you do that?'

When children approach the challenges and are able to reflect on their processes and procedures, they learn from one another's thinking mechanisms, plans and workings. And most importantly, they (and you) will learn from their mistakes. If they make mistakes when they apply, transpose and transform information during their workings, it gives you clues about what might need reinforcing. Simply marking an error and providing the correct answer for the child, won't drill down to correct a misconception.

Even if students are working on the same task, they can share what they found easy, what was tricky, how they overcame a particular hurdle, which processes or ideas did not serve them, which strategy they employed and how they would do it next time. They love to have ownership of their way of doing things.

'It was my idea to use the bottle cap to measure the exact amount of white paint.'

'Yes, and it was Ella's idea to use the cotton bud to get all the paint out, so that it was the whole amount, and none was left in the cap.'

During problem solving towards closed-ended goals, knowledge is mobilised. Addition is adding two numbers together to see how many elements there are. If this is not presented in a simple equation, but in the form of a word problem to solve, the operation must be evaluated and mobilised in the light of many distracting elements. Different operations will be identified in the language of the problem. For example:

Two sisters, Emma and Janet, had 10 lollies *each*. Emma's lollies were yellow, and Janet's lollies were pink. They shared *all* their lollies *among four* cousins who were visiting them. *How many* lollies did *each* of the visiting cousins get?

There is a procedure around problem solving:

- define the problem
- determine which elements are relevant
- visualise the steps
- sequence the steps
- enact the steps
- record the information
- reach the conclusion.

What do students need to competently define a problem? They need experience working with the problem, in a range of different ways. They can then begin to think like detectives, looking at the problem from different angles, assessing what they are dealing with in a more complete way. Decoding language is an important element of this detective work. For instance, in word problems, being alert to the kind of language that implies addition, subtraction, multiplication or division (or any other operation) is essential.

Problem-solving in this process involves pattern identification and recognising a recurring sequence. It is not practical to show an example of long division here, but if you are not familiar with the steps, I recommend you look it up. There is a pattern of actions. You multiply the divisor, you subtract the product from the whole dividend, you draw down the next digit, then you start over again. Within this problem-solving environment, you need to repeat the steps in a particular order to achieve the outcome. Long division also requires concepts of location. Where do you write the digits? Do you start your operation on the left or right? Do you write above or below the line? Not to mention, you must also monitor where you are in all of these complex processes along the way!

In the early years' classroom, we don't do long division, but students have innumerable opportunities to develop the network for generating, elaborating and using patterns. As they do this, they are developing the competence of holding information in short-term memory toward achieving a purpose. Some call this executive function.

While completing literacy tasks, students need to understand which language structure or format they are being asked to employ. In comprehension, they must monitor the narrative and follow a chronology which may not be presented in a linear way. The keywords in the question need to alert them to what they are meant to do as they solve a task. The question might be about an adult but relate to the age he was when he started school. In this case, the child will sort the information which relates to a character in separate time frames.

An example of an instruction about time sequence might be, 'Write a good paragraph using full sentences explaining the order that you do your morning routine'. (For younger children, ask them to draw it.)

The idea is to ensure students know and recognise how the language of setting closed-ended tasks acts as a guide for what they are meant to do.

To help children gain a more complete understanding, spending time unpacking problems into steps and evaluating efficiency together, becomes just as important as solving tasks correctly. Discovering different ways of doing things along the way builds flexibility into their thinking.

IN SUMMARY:

- closed-ended mobilisation involves setting tasks at various levels of challenge that have a known outcome
- solving the challenge may be direct and use one pathway, but where possible, look for ways to introduce flexibility and multiple ways to reach the solution
- students' problem-solving abilities improve when they are alerted to language cues intrinsic to how problems are framed
- it is important to break complex tasks down into steps and to sequence the steps overtly, before expecting children to employ them without discussion
- once children can identify the problem at hand, it's beneficial to interleave other different kinds of problems , as this will help them identify problems more fluently
- when students discuss their ideas, processes, mistakes, procedures, strategies, hurdles and possible improvement with others, it allows them to observe and use others' thoughts and methodologies to further build on what they know.

CHAPTER 14

Learning Zone 6 – Open-Ended Mobilisation

You don't think your way to creative work. You work your way to creative thinking.
George Nelson, Architect and Designer

Figure 38: Open-ended mobilisation

Coordinates

Open-ended mobilisation has the educator at three units and the students range at 35° (3:35°).

Definition

Open-ended mobilisation of knowledge is when students are inspired and encouraged to activate their curricular learning in novel and interesting ways. Going beyond where a concept, process, idea or symbol is understood, the task is to combine multiple elements towards an unrestricted outcome or destination. The goal is visualised by the individual student (or a collaborative group of students), to use, represent and communicate their knowledge in more individual ways than in closed-ended mobilisation. Students have a greater degree of freedom in how they acquire, capture, record and communicate their understanding. However, unlike the seventh zone that follows, there is not complete creative freedom, because the open-endedness still relates to set curriculum or project-based learning. As in closed-ended problem solving, the process students use to examine, design and achieve their goal, is of equal importance to the end result.

The educator's role involves:

- designing learning experiences using processes, resources and materials, which allow students to acquire, activate and communicate their knowledge in a variety of ways
- arranging the schedule and environment for individual or collaborative research and planning towards a visualised product or destination
- encouraging student to define, analyse, sequence and plan the steps to achieve and communicate their chosen path and destination
- encouraging students to apply, articulate and record their creative thinking, problem-solving strategies and procedures
- alerting students to the mental processes, routines and procedures they are using as they work towards open-ended goals
- emphasising flexibility and the testing of alternative means of reaching a creative goal
- assessing, recording and documenting the processes and procedures as they are implemented by the individual and the group to achieve their own outcomes.

The students' role involves:

- harnessing and applying their personal or collaborative knowledge in a unique way
- representing and communicating their learning and understanding in their own way
- developing appropriate plans and procedures and sequencing the steps to complete their self-designed tasks
- using appropriate language (verbal and/or non-verbal), to communicate their processes and outcomes
- deploying knowledge of concepts and applying it to achieving their visualised goal, generating a range of outcomes and products that demonstrate and communicate their understanding of learned concepts.

About open-ended mobilisation

In open-ended mobilisation, there is more freedom in the pathways, destinations, processes and communication of learning. There is still a curriculum goal for the learning, but the end-product is open-ended, giving students choice in the way they acquire, plan, traverse, reach and report their conceptual understanding.

I will use the example of a curriculum task presented by six teenage girls in a year nine literature classroom at an art, ballet, music and drama school where I began my career in education. I know it is out of our immediate age group, but the principle holds.

In the room, first one high, heavenly note trilling. Then a slow, sinuous fall into lower, fuller tones. The resonating voice advances and retreats. It rounds unexpectedly into haunting minor tones. The heart retracts and aches. The room seems to darken. Now new voices: from every corner, every space. Some high, some low, some long, some sighing, some a stuck, slow staccato. The chorus builds, assaulting the listener from every side. Then, each in its own time, the voices begin their retreat. Sequential silence. You feather down and settle as the last sound recedes ...

I was 'teaching' Samuel Taylor Coleridge's *Rime of the Ancient Mariner*, written as you might know, in a language that was not easily accessible to the group when they first encountered it. But we worked through it by creating access points from their own experience. In one part of Coleridge's epic poem, marooned sailors hear haunting voices in the air. I asked the girls who specialised in music if they would work together to enact these stanzas. Suffice to say, their performance exceeded my expectations. Their fellow students and I were transfixed by their work and their creativity. In a completely new way, the poem was 'taught' to me.

It was compulsory in the set curriculum to learn the poem, but we had freedom around how we could do it. Like closed-ended projects, open-ended tasks require procedures – the difference is, the exact outcome is unknown to everyone at the start. The unifying idea is the content learning you are endeavouring to cover.

If not with music, you can start in the early years with Unifix blocks. 'Use these Unifix blocks and teach me and your friends things you know about numbers.'

Let's go outside in the sunshine today and see what the shadows are doing

A school I visited a few years ago, could hardly get their students into the classrooms in the morning. Not one, but four, year levels of children from K4 though year 2, were infatuated with shadows. Not only the standard kind where an object blocks the sun, but an immense variety of different kinds of shadows and reflections.

The educators had been keen to introduce a science module in the Year One and Two groups and chose light and shadow because, as I've indicated before, it is a highly observable science.

The teachers didn't only rely on what was already in the outdoor space (like plants, play equipment, etc.) to cast shadows, they also strung up some washing lines between different poles and trees. They pegged up many different sizes and colours of laminated translucent paper like tissue paper, cellophane and patterned papers, some with shapes cut out of them. They strung up fabric in places where light was coming in from more than on direction. In one spot, light was coming from inside a building through a window into the playground and also directly from the sun. This complicated and multiplied the shadows.

The kids were more than excited about the density of the shadows, how dark they were, the multiplicity of shadows, the opacity, translucency and transparency of shadows. Amongst the coloured outdoor sheets and mobiles, there were also examples of foil and reflective surfaces.

The children involved in the project had younger siblings at the school and the younger children also got involved in the exploration.

In a safe concrete area as parents were dropping students to school, they saw kids drawing around others' shadows and recording their names within them. The plan was to come out later in the day, stand in the 'shadow footprints' and see where the shadows had moved to. In the classroom, children were invited to explain what they observed and to outline the kinds of experiments they wanted to do in the next week.

Figure 39: Light exploration

After several weeks of investigations, in the Year One and Year Two classes children were invited to use what they knew to do their own light projects. Some children wrote shadow plays and made shadow puppets; others created light collages with different materials on a light projector which they photographed for a 'light gallery'.

A group of children took photographs throughout the day and recorded the lengths and angles of the shadows as they moved. They produced a book 'A Story of Moving Shadows'.

One group of children, who had loved the coloured shadows, decided to choose five colours and give each a musical note. The music was played on resonator bells, which can be played like a xylophone, except each sound is a separate 'bell', so they can be handed out separately. The 'bells' are based on the pentatonic scale, where all the sounds are harmonious. So, any bell played in any order gave a lovely sound.

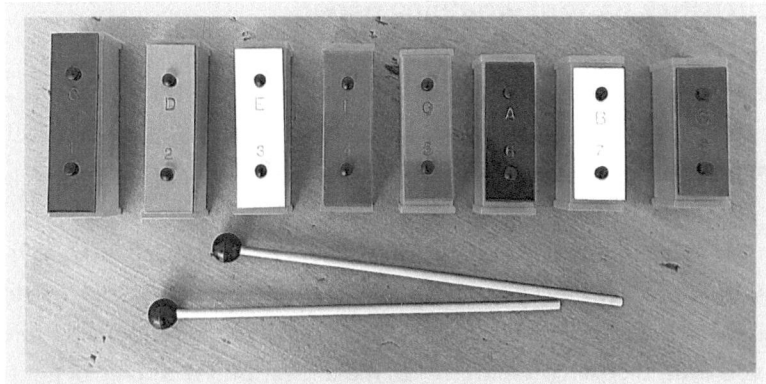

Figure 40: Resonator bells

The children had strips of coloured paper and lined them up in different orders to play the different melodies. Five children each had a bell and when their colour came up, they would play. There was a 'conductor' pointing at the 'notes'.

Someone suggested that the sounds could be repeated, so they cut out multiple strips of each colour, so a blue (or any other) colour's sound could be repeated several times before moving on to another sound. Another child suggested the music could be sped up or slowed down. How? The children inserted spaces between the paper strip notes which indicated more or less time before the next note. This added more variety to the compositions. One of the discoveries was that the melodies could be identically repeated if the patterns repeated. The music was recorded and could be replayed. It was an astounding project for year one and two children. It was musical composition using the arrangement of colour as notation. It controlled the pitch, pattern and timing of the melodies. And it was based on light!

There are many provocations to elicit creativity outside. What about the question: 'How can we get the wind to help us make beautiful sounds?'

Matchstick pattern wrapping paper

The creative projects don't need to be as extensive as the ones above. Like pop sticks, most classrooms have natural matchsticks (without the graphite flint of course).

'I'm giving everyone five matchsticks today. Make a pattern using all five and then draw it onto paper. When it is recorded, break your pattern and make and record a new one. When you've made as many patterns as you want to, use your patterns to make beautiful wrapping paper for family day next week. You can use any of the art materials in the studio to put your designs on the wrapping paper.'

In 1911, Sister Jane Erskine Stuart, an influential Catholic Educator wrote:

'...we are beginning to believe what has never ceased to be said, that lessons in lesson-books are not the whole of education ... the highest value

of all belongs to the things which children have made entirely themselves ... It is of greater value to a child to have grown one perfect flower than to have pulled many to pieces to examine their structure.' (Stuart 1911)

(Her book is free to read online through Gutenberg Press.)

You can collect evidence of learning during open-ended tasks when you track the concepts students are uncovering and putting to work. Their explanations may be more or less scientific to begin with and you want to allow them to use their own language. When they see the transformations as in the shadows above, they might describe the changes in position in their own way. The shadows hid in other shadows, the shadows were made with rainbows. The shadows grew longer/shorter and then moved to the right. Children don't need to know the exact angles, just observing the transformations sets them up for great thinking.

Great learning spills into the community

In several of the schools I have worked with in the past few years, students are making an impact beyond the classroom with their investigations. Children have been so passionate about environmental ideas that they have written to local councils asking if they can take responsibility for wildlife, and use parkland for observations, etc. One six-year-old child asked a restaurateur if he minded if she made and displayed a poster in his cafe window asking his customers to avoid single use plastic straws.

An example of this spilling into community with older children occurred when school averse boys in Year 10 were given the opportunity to base a project on their interests. They were parkour, or urban running, fanatics. They wrote about their sport and offered to give lessons to younger students in an area of the school where there was soft fill. Their project included physiology, nutrition, biomechanics and statistics. They were really keen to have an area where they themselves could train in this incredible sport. They wrote to their local council and were invited to give a presentation. On the basis of that, the council allocated a seven-figure sum of money to build walls and provide soft fill in a local park!

This is education that is truly alive.

IN SUMMARY:

- open-ended mobilisation has a curriculum goal, but the learning pathway and assessment tasks are, to a degree, unknown to either the educator/s or the students at the beginning of the investigation
- the products in this zone can be broad and achieved over a substantial amount of time, or small and completed within a single session or day
- creative products often combine elements from different disciplines, for example, science and music
- the educator is a facilitator and provides materials and scaffolds to help children to refine their understanding in employing concepts
- evidence can be collected in a variety of ways including recording conversations and using digital means like video, photography or audio recording.

CHAPTER 15

Learning Zone 7 – Auto-Generative Creativity

You can't use up creativity. The more you use the more you have.
Maya Angelou

The world is as many times new as there are children in our lives.
Robert Brault, Freelance Writer

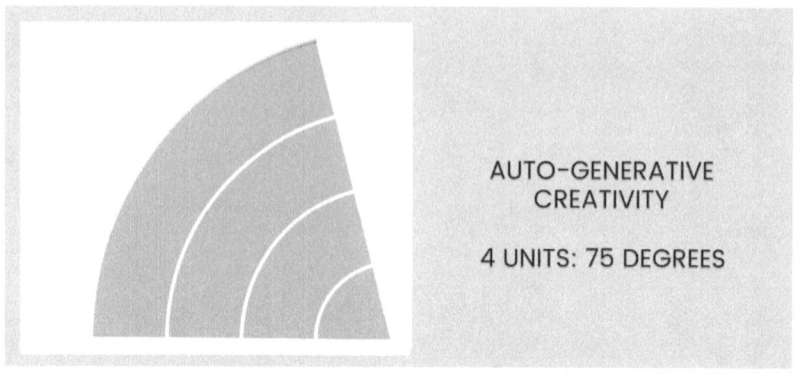

Figure 41: Auto-generative creativity

Coordinates

This zone is at the maximum distance: four units with a range of 75° (4:75°).

Definition

Auto-generative creativity is when a task, goal or activity is initiated in the mind of an individual. It might or might not relate to curriculum learning. It could occur as a unique way of viewing current information and originating a new perspective or significance. It could occur as a new technique for doing something. Or, it may be the first time a person has discovered and used something that is known to the world but new to the individual. Once the creative intention, visualisation or action is in the world, it can be shared and used in a collaborative way with others. The creativity is sometimes born in the mind, but it can equally emerge in a state of flow as when a child is immersed in painting, or an adult is working with processes and materials. Creativity can occur without external influences, or it can be facilitated as a result of creative prompts.

The educator's role involves:

- harnessing his or her own interests, passions, learnings and ideas in creative ways in the classroom
- being overtly respectful of creative ideas and actions students bring to conceptual understanding
- recognising the auto-generative creativity of students
- encouraging students' self-generative activity and products to launch more advanced learning
- facilitating and guiding the creative process as it is underway, lending skills or providing access to more materials
- providing opportunities to imagine and generate creative ideas
- recognising instances of auto-generative creativity and attuning students to their own creative intuition and processes.

The students' role involves:

- spontaneously accessing and using a variety of skills, knowledge and processes when approaching a self-projected task
- developing a product that is unique to them and may be unique to the world
- being independent and capable of designing tasks but may also confer with others in collaborative ways to solve problems or develop products.

When children enact their auto-generative creativity, we have made ourselves redundant, and that is when we have done our best job.

About auto-generative creativity

In truth, the coordinate dimension of this zone was only enumerated to fit it into the graphic of the Agility Wheel. Creativity is infinite.

However, it is not necessarily automatic. We must develop a mindset to activate creativity. And sometimes, if we follow the writings of Edward de Bono, we have to work at it.

In a classroom where children's ideas, products, offerings and wisdom are ignored, devalued or subverted, they won't learn to use their independent thinking and their creative force.

The classroom nuisance

While visiting a school, I took a 15-minute tea break to check my emails in a small room along a corridor. A seven-year-old lad sidled up to me, with a barrage of questions.

'Who are you? Are you coming back into our classroom? What are you doing? Can I play a game on your iPad?'

I answered the questions, then added, no, he couldn't really use my iPad because he was meant to be with his mates in his classroom with his teacher.

'I don't want to go back, and anyway, I only come to school to be the classroom nuisance.'

Ummmmm. Flip! I think to myself. How is this for a self-fulfilling Pygmalion moment!

'Really? Don't you like learning?'

'Na, I want to stay home and play with my Pokémon.'

'Tell me about Pokémon.'

He tells me how many cards he has, his favourite and least favourite characters. He talks about the video game, the health and damage he has to quantify for his characters as they journey through the game. He knows the value of the different trainers and characters. He talks about several characters' skills in attacks and their battle superpowers. He talks about the levels Pokémon evolve through: when Charmander receives enough experience from battles, it evolves into Charmeleon, and later Charizard. (And there are evolutions beyond that!)

His knowledge of the characters, the statistics, the narratives is complex. The memory about the characters, where they belong in the catalogue, what he still wants to collect and his combined knowledge of the video game and the card collecting is impressive.

In no way is this a kid who doesn't like learning. He just has not been switched on to learning *in school*.

If he is already outside the learning at seven, how is he going to get through the rest of it?

Classroom creators

At a school I'd visited earlier in the same week, three six-year-old boys were ensconced in a small room set off their main classroom constructing a model of the human heart. They were using a heart shaped chocolate box, tubing for blood vessels and were thinking about how the heart pumps blood because 'it is a very strong muscle'. It was part of an open-ended investigation into the human body.

In the large classroom children were learning about their hands using three modalities, drawing, writing and digital photography. One child had written, '*I need hands so that I can hold a spoon. Evry (sic) one has lines on their hands. We can feel with our hands and we can eat with our hands.*' This was May in Prep! He then photographed his writing, and his realistic drawing with an iPad. He added a few images from a safe search engine to illustrate his information. No adult prompted his actions which included self-correcting an error in his writing!

There were individual representations of the skeletal system on the walls where children had used earbuds, grass straw, matchsticks and many other materials to replicate human bone structure. For most of the lesson (which extended for a couple of hours, not 45 minutes) the children were working independently or in small groups with access to an endless array of materials … And not one was labelled a nuisance.

What inspired you?

Think about your own teachers at school. Which of them do you remember with the most fondness and respect? Which experiences over the course of your education do you think were formative, influencing your thinking and creativity. Perhaps a gifted teacher even had a hand in who you imagined you might become, or which pathway your education would take?

To be creative, you need knowledge. The broader and deeper the knowledge the better. But you also need encouragement and inspiring models who enact their own creativity.

Creativity can occur at any moment and at any level within a school day. I have mentioned before the child who made the folded puppets. She is also the child who imagined herself sewing wings and who made a 3D card, where a rolled-up column of paper popped up when she opened it. I can still visualise her giggling uproariously every time she did it. If we are not on the look-out for auto-generative creativity, we might not see it. If we don't value students' independent, creative ideas and products, they might stop offering them.

Creativity occurs in different ways. A child might discover something for themselves before realising that it is 'a thing' in the real world. They notice that when they mistakenly plaster some red paint on the yellow paint, boom bang, orange emerges. Of course, paint mixing is well-known in the world, but this is their personal discovery of it. If they employ it, it is their first creative use of it. Creativity does not have to be something completely new to the world or entirely original. It has to be new and original to us.

Within the framework of the routines and curricular activity, a world of knowing and wondering is revealed. To return to the late Loris Malaguzzi's tenet that children have a hundred languages to express themselves, the use of the various means as described in the classroom above creates the environment where creation can germinate and flourish.

The underlying reason for this is that all the sensory modalities are engaged, which enhances learning. The hundred languages harness the auditory, visual and kinaesthetic modalities of learning. This idea also resonates with Howard Gardner's theory of multiple intelligences (Gardner 1993).

To facilitate these languages, emphasis is placed on providing an environment which is rich in possibilities, and which aims to engage children's interest and experience. There is an endless offering of variety within the security of predictable routine. A normality of latent possibility.

The children use these languages not only to demonstrate their knowledge, but also to construct knowledge. The same brain function which enables us to remember and organise information from the environment, also enables us to create.

A glimpse into the creative brain

The human brain, a most miraculous organ, fascinates me. Sir Charles Sherrington, Nobel prize-winner and the grandfather of neurophysiology said that when the brain fires, 'It is as if the Milky Way entered on some cosmic dance' (Sherrington 1955).

Each human brain has in excess of one million, million brain cells – 1000 000 000 000. When a thought is triggered, each individual brain cell is capable of contacting and embracing as many as 10 000 *or more* proximate brain cells. When they communicate, the number of possible combinations in the brain if written out would be one followed by 10.5 million kilometres of noughts! (Buzan 2010)

The brain is the only organ that is mostly formed by interaction with experiences external to it. It is literally created by experience. To be helpful, the experience needs to be positive. When you're labelled a nuisance, the learning happens equally well, just negatively.

The more often repeated the experience is, the more efficient memory and thought becomes. Each repetition results in myelination, the creation of an overlay of a white fatty substance that augments the speed of neural networks. The way to encourage myelination in the brains of our students is to use the following six principles:

1. We learn through all our senses
2. We remember well what happened at the beginning (primacy)
3. We remember well what happened at the end (recency)
4. We remember what we are interested in
5. We remember new things we can connect to what is already known
6. We remember things that engage our emotions (Buzan & Buzan 1993).

Each of these principles can be harnessed to support students' creativity.

The genesis of curriculum content and possible projects

I would like to shift the conversation from students' creativity to your own creativity. You are the most important resource in your role as an educator. You are the archetypal auto-generator.

My educational practice is a function of my lived experience and there are so many things I love to do. In my seminars and consultations, I always advise educators to bring their whole selves to the table. If you love patchwork, gardening, astronomy, historical bottle digging, keeping chickens, model aeroplanes, dirt biking, scrapbooking or anything else ... bring it!

I have the tremendous fortune to travel a lot. (It seems a distant memory at this moment, as I sit writing this in Melbourne in the middle of the COVID lockdown!)

When I travel I am always on the lookout. My paternal grandmother (who always planted a fig tree the minute she moved anywhere!) used to say, 'Lil, you can steal with your eyes'.

I've done this all my life. If I see, do, feel or newly understand anything that inspires me, it has the potential to inspire others. So, I consciously curate memories and experiences I can draw on for planning curricula inquiries. Perhaps it's William Blake's illustrations at the Tate Gallery in London, Richard Serra's immense sculptures at the Guggenheim museum, Bilbao, Andy Goldsworthy's phenomenal ephemeral artworks in nature (Goldsworthy 1989), or the recent exceptional 'Alice in Wonderland' mixed media exhibition at ACMI in Melbourne in 2019.

I love Federation Square – so much so, that I based an educational project on it with my colleague, Marg Campbell in 2005 called 'Line Dance'. Federation Square is the most eclectic collection of lines you can imagine: architectural, mathematical and natural. The project crossed multiple disciplines and captured hundreds of ways *line* is meaningful to children and to society. I think it is still my favourite exploration ever.

In 2019, I had the exceptional joy and honour of convening a public exhibition of Reggio Emilia-inspired contributions from 10 schools, 'Reimagining Children, Spaces and Relationships', held in the Atrium at Federation Square (the piazza of Melbourne). Within my role at Independent Schools Victoria (ISV), my colleague Helen Schiele and I were stewards of a 'Thinker in Residence' program with Curtin University Senior Lecturer, Dr Stefania Giamminuti, as 'thinker'. We worked alongside the 10 schools for three to four years and the exhibition was a culmination of that collaborative work.

The exhibition was the early years' component of ISV's second biannual Arts Learning Festival. This groundbreaking festival crosses education sectors and international boundaries and celebrates *unlimited imagination*. The festival honours the importance of arts in education and facilitates events for schools, students, families and the wider community. The exhibition was achieved in partnership with the Reggio Emilia Australian Information Exchange (REAIE) and included bringing to Australia two remarkable speakers: Paola Strozzi and Filippo Ciele from the Reggio Children organisation. The value of this endeavour was in the number and range of people brought together in a significant creative collaboration.

Let's move from my love of Federation Square back to planning!

To commence curricular planning, with everything I love and everything that interests me in the background, I use Tony Buzan's six prompts above and his mind-mapping process and put down everything I know about the idea I seek to explore. I gather everything my friends and colleagues know. I read up, go online, look for visuals and watch videos. I go out and take photographs, I visit the places I might want to take children, I contact the experts I want to invite.

Then the real planning begins. I usually map out my ideas for the different ways a project can be explored across the arts, sciences and particularly movement and performance arts. Once all that is set out, I search for a beginning.

The first encounter with ideas and materials is what will ignite the children's interest (the primacy effect). It was not unusual for me to spend half the night setting up an installation for the beginning of a project, and then taking it down the next night because, as you all well know, the space is needed by someone else the day after! But it was always worth it. One of the extremely important things about it, is documenting the encounter. The photographs, video, conversations and responses of the children are fuel for later discussions, when the learning is unpacked more deeply.

Whether it is medieval, outer space, light and shadow, or things that roll, there should be a good beginning. And the beginnings don't all have to be productions. The early introductions of the Explorations Project were just well-placed hands-on experiences that were in the room for two to three weeks before we even discussed them. We just observed what the children did with ice, how they used the water play area and their experimentation with pipettes placed beside jars of coloured water and sheets of blotting paper. These explorations were prefiguring the later, deeper and more complex work to come.

The end of projects is also important. They might be the performance on the day you have family visitors, or a special celebration like Harmony Day or Footy Day. You could have a book launch or show a film at a red-carpet event. While working at a school in 2000, we had a mini-Olympics to coincide with the Sydney Olympics. Each year level explored a sport or some aspect of the iconic Olympic movement. My group was immersed in the long jump – and they loved it. We had our own team emblem, flag, mascots and class long jump records. It was a blast!

In between a good start and a good end, the senses, interests, and adding to prior knowledge just happen. Even the enhancement of children's conceptual knowledge!

The brain can transport us to other places, other times and other possibilities. We can create what never existed before.

The school is not only a place for transmitting culture, but for creating it. We can create a culture that supports creativity. We should all endeavour to create and maintain a culture of respect for children and their innate ability to construct their learning with us. They will interpret and change the world as they become the builders of the future.

It is our task to guide towards many metamorphoses.

In Reggio Emilia they have a saying: 'Nothing without Joy!' It is a mantra I have always found energising and inspiring.

IN SUMMARY:

- auto-generative creativity is when students or educators use prior and newly acquired knowledge to solve a problem in a unique way or design a product that is unique to them or to the world
- a culture of respecting creativity will allow it to flourish
- when students have assimilated and can independently mobilise, deploy, and use knowledge they have gained, we are made redundant. Our job is done.

CHAPTER 16

The Edu-Chameleon

Intelligence is the handmaiden of flexibility and change.
Vernor Vinge, A Fire Upon the Deep

Often throughout this book, I have spoken about knowing things well first and then using the knowledge in unique and flexible ways across different contexts later. This is transfer.

Having outlined seven distinctive learning zones, I now ask that you *not* only see them individually. Of course, you can plan to use a zone consciously and implement it on its own. But, at any moment, in any zone, you can engage what you know about another zone. This is often referred to as incidental teaching. You know about incidental teaching, and I'm sure you've used it. But with clear knowledge of each zone, the repertoire for your educational action and intervention increases in range.

In the middle of free play, a child shows you a leaf. Some people say, 'That's nice, honey'. You recognise the learning opportunity. Do you engage the zone of mediated play, or even clarity of concept for the duration of your conversation? Do you make a note of the interaction because in the curriculum you are planning a life sciences investigation? Do you suggest the child collects a few more leaves to put on the light table for wax crayon rubbings on translucent paper? Do you notice that the leaves around you provide a perfect matching, sorting and counting activity? Which way will you turn? Where do you pivot?

When you know the zones well, you can instantly recognise and harness opportunities for each kind of learning.

Pivoting between giving children range and narrowing the focus is calibrating between independent learning, mediated learning and scripted learning. For children to move upwards through zones of proximal development, they need all of these. They need to be challenged continuously, but at the appropriate level and in a way that keeps their minds active.

The Edu-Chameleon is at the centre of the Agility Wheel. He or she can consciously deploy a learning zone and also be ready to pivot in an instant if it is immediately beneficial for an individual or group of children. This is the creative use of your knowledge, competence and skills.

Conversation about creativity

Creativity has always been a departure point of this book – not to be limited by a binary paradigm. Edward de Bono says (surprisingly) that 'the brain is not designed to be creative'. He presents the notion that creativity can be engendered by 'deliberate and systematic techniques that can be used in a formal manner' (De Bono 1993).

We have to wake our brains up and move them out of patterns of thinking, routines, habitual behaviour and even the appreciation of the known, tried and tested.

I once had an interview with the principal of a prestigious private school to present a project on developing students' metacognition and personalising learning. The principal listened, then responded that the ideas were highly appealing, but that the school was running too well, the parents were too happy and the students were achieving enviable results. There was no reason to fix what was working well.

There is absolutely nothing wrong with that.

But I would like to put a spanner in the works, just for your consideration.

To do that, I am offering you a quartet of prompts for creative thinking:

- A Bird's Eye View
- A Maze
- A Branch
- The Ladder of Aspiration

These prompts are completely open-ended, and you can apply them in any way or in any context you wish to.

A Bird's Eye View

In relation to the Bird's Eye View prompt, let's return to the principal who loved the idea of innovation, but was very comfortable about the school's performance, and unwilling to implement any changes.

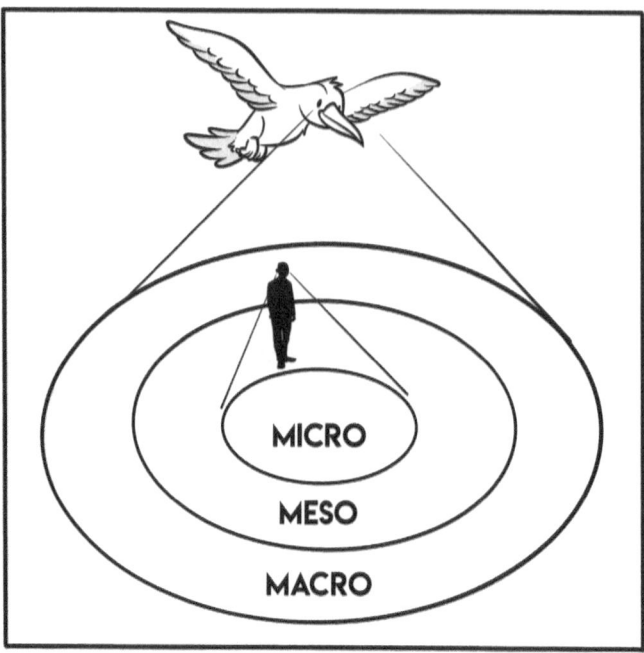

Figure 42: Bird's Eye View

When something is running really well, it can be because you've been doing it for ages, and it works. You have your 46 boxes packed and ready to break open every week. Or, it can be because you have periodically put your head up, surveyed the landscape, and *continue to evaluate* it as the best way to run your process. You still believe that your students' outcomes and achievements are current and valuable.

What you are doing every day, can be characterised as a micro landscape. It is set within a broader landscape, the macro environment.

There are many influential forces at work in the macro environment. They have the power to impact on the micro word in the immediate term, in the medium term and in the long term. An example of an influence in the immediate term is the disruption of COVID-19 on global education. Because of its urgency, it could not be ignored. Other forces are not as visible, and an effort needs to be made to identify what might be shaping things from beyond the micro space.

The Bird's Eye View prompt encourages you to expand your perspective every so often to assess what is happening in your micro environment, in relation to current and emerging macro forces.

We will have a look at this at the corporate, educator and student levels.

Corporate viewpoint

The forces from the macro environment are regularly summarised by the term PESTLE, thought to have originated by the Harvard professor Francis Aguilar in the 1960s. The model refers to the constellation of forces below:

- Political
- Economic
- Social
- Technical
- Environmental
- Legal

Some organisations assessing shaping forces adapt this model and include additional areas that are important to them. One inclusion I think is necessary is ethical, so you might think about it as STEEPLE. I also like to extend Social to Socio-Cultural because it implies a recognition of inclusive practice.

Any place of education needs to take notice of what is happening in the macro space.

In the Bird's Eye View, there are three concentric circles: micro, meso and macro. There is a figure in the centre with a circumscribed vision.

There is bird hovering with a much broader perspective. The prompt is asking for us to broaden our perspective to refine our decision-making, as well as our current (and particularly) our future practice.

In this way, if you notice something on the horizon that indicates you should transform some elements of your micro world, you can start to work on it. For it not to be too disruptive, the creativity prompt provides a meso space. A place in between your streamlined micro efficiency, and the direct impact of the macro world.

Your meso space becomes a space for research and pre-planning. If you are a leader, you might like to offer reading materials or professional learning opportunities to key members of staff. You might create an innovative teacher research project within routine practice to assess the impact of the new ideas. If the outcomes of the research are positive, the meso space is where you plan the means to disrupt the micro environment and bring your community on board to the new thinking.

I have seen this in operation at a school with multiple year levels. Leaders in the early years' arena implemented changes via mini research projects. When parents were startled by changes they saw in the classroom, they complained. The school leadership asked for things to return to the old 'normal'.

But the innovative early years' educators stood their ground and asked for the grace of time. For a few months they tracked maths and literacy competency using the same assessment tools they had in the past. They compared the new normal results against old normal results, and were able to present evidence of improvement.

Over time the research in the early years saw transformations in practice from the infant rooms, through the primary and middle school, to secondary staff and students. The conceptualisation of the role of the educator, the image of students and the image of leadership changed dramatically.

The parents were brought on board – and it is now a principle that early communication with parents, and even parent involvement in decision-making in some endeavours, has changed the relationship between the school and the community.

Work in the meso space can have an enormous impact on the micro space. It can be done with well-considered intention. Evidence can be collected and tracked. It is possible to address the forces from the macro environment in a manageable, staged way.

The educator viewpoint

This broadening of perspective does not only occur at the institutional level. You can apply it to your personal practice, or if you are lucky enough to work within a collaborative professional learning team, to a small group of colleagues.

The idea is to give yourself permission to explore, research and implement transformations in a manageable, fluid and trackable way. You might like to investigate new techniques, so you learn about them and plan how to implement and include them into what you are already doing. You have a play in the meso space. This might be reading, listening to others or visiting. The visit can be as simple as going into your colleague's teaching spaces, or it might be to another school, state or even another country!

The student viewpoint

When you assess students, you make assumptions and come to conclusions about your immediate observations. But you can implement the Bird's Eye View in relation to the student too.

The PESTLE model for students might be:

- Performance
- Emotional
- Social
- Technical
- Language
- Experimental

Rather than relying on surface observations, expand your perspective to consider more than what meets the eye.

A student's performance (P) relates to the entire way the child is integrated into the learning space. It is the combination of how they perform on tasks, their ability to deal with routine and change, their interactions with others and their general attitude to learning.

If you want to check in to see how any of these elements might be enhanced, you can ask yourself questions about what might be affecting the child's emotional energy (E) or social competence (S). Technical (T) refers to where they are in their skill levels for a task, whether it is how to cut with scissors, or how to structure a problem-solving task. Assess their facility with language (L). Have they consolidated a concept, are they ready for more complex language? Or are they battling because the main language is not their home language? Do they need coaching in how to express their feelings or information? Don't forget to tune into body language and their tone when they communicate because that is often where you will see what is really happening. All of these questions will prompt ideas about how you can structure change for the child.

The experimental (E) part is the creation of a mini research project in which you hypothesise about the implementation of a strategy.

An example from my own practice was that a child who had elements of Asperger's syndrome had difficulty staying on task during the day. I implemented a short 10-minute planning session with him before the doors opened each day. Together we discussed and drew the tasks and then the plan was put in his locker. Whenever he lost his way or motivation, we could refer back to the map. I also left periods of the day free for him to follow his own path. The partnership in pre-planning, the interleaving of planned and unplanned time and the consistency all had powerfully positive results in his performance.

It is important to apply this kind of thinking to every student. Sometimes our focus is so riveted on children who are battling in some way that we forget to enhance the performance of children ready for a rise in their zone of proximal development.

The Maze

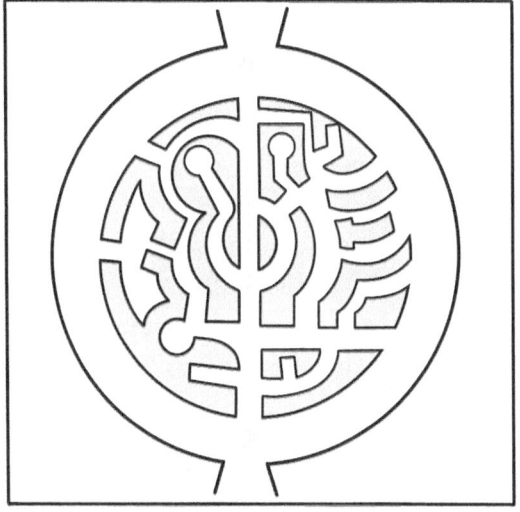

Figure 43: The maze

PESTLE invites you to look outward to see what is impacting your profession and your practice. The Maze is an internal landscape. It invites you to pause and reflect inwardly on where you are and where you might want to be. There is a direct route through the maze representing a clear and simple path from here to there. If you are totally comfortable that you are on the right track, you can ignore everything else about the maze. We have times like this in our lives, when we are in flow and the road seems clear.

But if your vision is not that clear, you might like to pause for a moment in the maze. Is there something you want to do to clarify your goals? Do you want to spend more time deepening your knowledge about yourself, your practice and your environment before you move forward? Is there something else you want to be doing in your life? Does where you are suit your values, your sense of self and your aspirations? If there are parts of the internal maze that don't serve you, that are fruitless dead ends, close them off.

Not all dead ends are bad. There are some termini where you might like to spend some time and just enjoy the scenery. These cul-de-sacs might not lead you through the maze but are valuable in themselves.

There is also often more than one way out of the maze towards your goals than the direct route alone.

Robert Frost ponders over 'The Road Not Taken'. If you take a chance and head down a different path, you will learn to navigate its challenges and intricacies. The diversion can add to your expertise, knowledge and wisdom.

The maze is an invitation to authentically check in to your internal space to see if you want to trek directly ahead or take a diversion – even if you don't exactly know where it will take you. This kind of deep reflection may prompt you to stay where you are, or you might realise you want to be somewhere else. Consider the road not taken.

The Branch

Figure 44: The Branch

The branch is a prompt about seeing connection. Say you pick up a leaf and it is labelled with the word 'grit'. How do you interpret it?

You pick up another leaf and it reads 'soccer ball'.

A third leaf is labelled, 'compression'.

Take a moment and try to make some connections.

You will definitely be able to, because our brain is constantly trying to make sense of things so it can know them and turn them into comfortable, predicable pieces of information. If we don't make these connections, information exists as a standalone piece of knowledge. It is not part of a bigger picture. We want children to see how things cohere. We want them to have both a big picture view as well as the details.

The three words I offered, grit, soccer ball and compression will make more sense if I explain where they come from. The Branch prompt has a main branch which is a content focus. It divides into two boughs to represent the adoption of two different disciplines to explore the content.

I wanted to use a completely abstract idea as the starting point for content, so in the middle of a walk with a friend, I came up with the word 'bounce'. If you had the word as a content provocation, where would it take you? Write down one or two ideas before I relate my own.

'Bounce' suggested two areas of exploration for me. The first was the laws of physics, and the second was the concept of resilience.

If we go the physics route, the work with children can be really fun and exciting.

They can be offered several different kinds of objects to explore their bouncing properties. They can talk about how the different effort they apply when they bounce a particular ball can change the height of the bounce. The direction you bounce the ball can change where it bounces to. They will be exploring an object's ability to return to its original shape after being stretched or squeezed. An example I researched online used a rubber ball, a ping pong ball and a marble (Education.com 2020).

You can provide any number of materials and children can imagine what it is that makes things bounce. Whether they actually reach the point of using the language of compression, elasticity and latent energy is not really that important. The process of observing, planning, predicting and hypothesising is good enough.

If they understand the properties of bouncing back after a bump, it takes us to the other discipline, the psychology of mindset. Having grit, is the ability to bounce back and be resilient. To return to form after something has stretched or bounced you out of shape!

Understanding grit, soccer ball and compression together, rather than as isolated ideas, gives the investigation its coherence.

We want to spend time on the leaves and have multiple leaves; but we want to know that the information is connected at a deeper, more coherent level.

What other abstract ideas can you generate as provocations for learning?

The Ladder of Aspiration

Figure 45: The ladder of aspiration

I think the ladder image is very clear. What do you want to achieve? And what are the four steps you can immediately put in place to get you there. It is not to say that the steps can be instantly achieved, but as you rise up one step, you will know what the next part of the process it.

The image was designed with a wall in the background. This suggests that you most likely won't be able to see what is over the wall as an outcome of your aspirations. What I have found over time, is that the more I aspire to develop my knowledge and expertise, the more interesting the vista over the wall becomes.

I have provided you with space to write your four steps in this book. If you have the e-version, it will be in the downloadable PDF that accompanies the book. Make a commitment now, to yourself.

I have often heard the disparaging comment that 'those who can't do, teach'. It has always made me furious. I don't think there is a more noble profession than being a stepping stone for students to reach their aspirations in life. So look for those around you that inspire and are stepping stones for you.

Don't play small with you aspirations. When Nelson Mandela came out of prison, he quoted the American author, Marianne Williamson. And the quote is one that I have displayed in every room or study where I have ever worked.

> 'Our deepest fear is not that we are inadequate. Our deepest fear is that we are powerful beyond measure. It is our light, not our darkness that most frightens us. We ask ourselves, 'Who am I to be brilliant, gorgeous, talented, fabulous?' Actually, who are you not to be? You are a child of God. Your playing small does not serve the world. There is nothing enlightened about shrinking so that other people won't feel insecure around you. We are all meant to shine, as children do. We were born to make

manifest the glory of God that is within us. It's not just in some of us; it's in everyone. And as we let our own light shine, we unconsciously give other people permission to do the same. As we are liberated from our own fear, our presence automatically liberates others.'

When you plan your four steps, see them as four stepping stones to a new you. A you that is more educated, more influential, more well-rounded and closer to who you are destined to be in this life.

Uncover the edu-chameleon in you

The absolute basis of this book is to scaffold children's conceptual understand from an early age. To engage their minds and imagination at the level that is appropriate to their current zone of proximal development and which also paves the way for future learning.

I know that you will continue to aspire to new goals in your practice and I encourage you to embrace the edu-chameleon in you. Dare to explore the endless possibilities and potential for joy and learning available in the everyday, and over the years, in a myriad of ways. Your role as an educator is vitally important and I wish you immense success.

PART D

The Tail – Edu-Chameleon Lists

No weapons are more potent than brevity and simplicity.
Katherine Cecil Thurston

In this part you will find a collection of edu-chameleon lists that can act as references to assist you to achieve the goals discussed throughout the book.

As we know, Brendan Bartlett sees the list as a useful language structure. I hope you find them useful too!

Edu-chameleon lists:

- 13 universal relationships
- 20 key concepts for organising knowledge and eliciting meaning
- A dozen thinking skills
- 5 senses words
- Weather words
- 10 modalities for learning
- Play ideas and equipment
- Social, emotional and cultural concepts and skills
- Gross and fine motor skills
- Social interactions
- Emotional intelligence (EQ)
- Curriculum areas to explore: arts and crafts, science and nature, mathematics and verbal literacy.

13 Universal Relationships

It is through relationships that everything in the universe coheres. The relationships largely answer the grand old questions starters: *Who, What, Where, When, How and Why?* After reviewing the 13 universal relationships for all levels of learning in the table below, take a moment to pause and reflect on Rudyard Kipling's enduring poem, *I Keep Six Honest Serving-Men*.

Qualifying	What/who is it?
Analytical	How can it be analysed into whole and parts? (The opposite is synthesis.)
Functional	How does it work? What makes it work? And why?
Temporal	When is it placed in sequence and time?
Spatial	Where is it located or related in space?
Comparative	How is it similar, equivalent or different? And why?
Causal	What is the cause and effect? And why?
Dependent	What depends on what? And why?
Transformational	How and what has changed and why?
Quantifying	How is it estimated or measured for precision and accuracy?
Hypothetical	If something happens what might follow? And why?
Imaginative	Wondering what, where, when, how and why something might be.
Ethical	What is whose responsibility to something?

I keep six honest serving-men
(They taught me all I knew);
Their names are What and Why and When
And How and Where and Who.
I send them over land and sea,
I send them east and west;
But after they have worked for me,
I give them all a rest.

I let them rest from nine till five,
For I am busy then,
As well as breakfast, lunch, and tea,
For they are hungry men.
But different folk have different views;
I know a person small
She keeps ten million serving-men,
Who get no rest at all!
She sends em abroad on her own affairs,
From the second she opens her eyes
One million Hows, Two million Wheres,
And seven million Whys!

Rudyard Kipling – The Elephant's Child

20 Key Concepts for Organising Knowledge and Eliciting Meaning

Super-ordinate Concept	Elements that belong to the concept
1. colour	This could be explored through the colours themselves: red, blue, yellow, green, purple, orange, violet, indigo, black and white; or the features: primary, secondary, pastel, shade, hue, light, dark, tone
2. dimension	These include length, width, height, area, volume, weight, density, speed, volume (sound), distance, pressure, angles, temperature, wavelength, interval and unit.
3. distance	Some examples related to distance include metric, kilometres, imperial, miles and light-years.
4. emotion	There are many emotions, each with multiple associated labels. For example, happy, sad, angry, excited, surprised, fearful and disgusted. It is important for students to be able to distinguish both the broad and subtle differences in emotions.
5. form	Forms that are not Euclidian shapes are included here: bulbous, thorny, tentacled, etc. Each example needs to be examined and described. There are some wonderful natural forms such as symmetrical, radiant, divergent, convergent, pinnate, linear, spiral, concentric, webbed, tessellated and fractal to name a few.

6.	function	Functions are individual to entities, so need to be assessed in situ. Look at the internal workings and external impact of any object, entity or system. Examples are transport, measurement, locomotion, recording sound, mixing food, etc.
7.	length	Units of measurements including metric, millimetre, centimetre, metre, kilometre, imperial, inch, foot, yard and mile.
8.	location	There are lots of variations here, such as above, around, at, back, before, behind, below, beside, centre, down, far, front, in, inner, left, middle, near, next to, north, on top, on, out, outer, right, south, underneath, up and within.
9.	material	A huge variation of elements can be examined here such as concrete, cork, glass, leather, metal, natural materials, paper, Perspex, plastic, polystyrene, porcelain, rubber, shell, sponge, stone and wood.
10.	orientation	Generally, orientation refers to the universal directions and coordinates we use to locate ourselves in space: north, south, east, west, (plus all the in between measures), as well as longitude and latitude.
11.	pattern	Any identifiable recurring trend. Patterns can be labelled, e.g. ABAB, ABBA, AABBCC etc. Patterns can also be seen in materials, and in all the phenomena around us, like the cycles of the moon, seasons, etc. We can see patterns of behaviour and many other kinds. These patterns also relate to the forms above.

12.	perspective	Similar to orientation, perspective is the position you view things from. This can be physical perspective, but also attitudinal, psychological, social, political and other perspectives. Students benefit from learning about perspective in a variety of ways.
13.	senses	Sight, hearing, smell, taste and touch all have concepts related to them. We can also refer to our inward senses and intuitions. See the senses table that follows.
14.	shape	**One-dimensional linear shape:** crenelated, curved, parallel, round, straight, wavy **Two-dimensional shapes (geometric):** diamond, dodecagon, hexagon, octagon, parallelogram, pentagon, polygon, quadrilateral, rectangle, rhombus, square, triangle **Curved Shapes:** arc, circle, ellipse, oval, parabola **Three dimensional shapes:** cone, cube, cylinder, polyhedrons (3D shapes with straight sides), prism, pyramid, sphere and torus (like a donut).
15.	size	Wide ranging including, diminutive, microscopic, miniscule, minute, small, medium, middling, midsized, regular, colossal, enormous, huge, large and massive.
16.	speed	Lots of possibilities beyond the usual fast and slow, such as cadence, dashing, hastening, hurried, hurtling, moderate, motoring, rate, rhythm, sedate, slow-moving, steady, whizzing and zooming.
17.	temperature	Again, plenty of choices beyond the obvious including ambient, baking, blistering boiling, Celsius, chilly, cold, degrees, Fahrenheit, freezing frosty, heat, icy, tepid, thermal, thermometer and warm.

18. time	From specific measurements to concepts, there is a multitude of ways to introduce an explore time, such as: 12 hours, 24 hours, afternoon, age, always, am, annual, biannual, century, contemporaneous, contemporary, continual, continuous, dawn, day, decade, dusk, early, eon, era, evening, future, half hour, hour, late, midday, millennium, millisecond, minute, moment, month, morning, never, new, night, now, old, past, permanent, pm, present, quarter hour, second, soon, temporary, then, today, tomorrow, week, year, yesterday and young.
19. volume	This can be further examined using elements like litre, millilitre, pint, quart, etc.
20. weight	There are lots of opportunities to explore here too, including heavy, light, gram, milligram, kilogram, ounce, pound and stone.

A Dozen Thinking Skills

1. **Focus and attention**
   No learning can take place without focus and attention. It implies self-regulation. Attention may be directed to a single object or a complex task. Irrelevant stimuli are ignored. When there is complex field, focus needs to be directed in a systematic way to gather all relevant information (often left to right, or top to bottom).

2. **Labelling**
   Language is the essential toolkit for thinking and learning. Precise meaning should be attached to each label. Labels denote phenomena in both the concrete and abstract domains. They can be contextual. Labels apply to simple and compound ideas (like electro-magnetism). All parts of the compound idea need to be understood. Labels may be understood in receptive language before they are readily articulated in expressive language.

3. **Spatial perception**
   This is a relational understanding of position and orientation. Each object is positioned or oriented in relation to something else. Spatial perception involves different points of view. Some spatial information is informed from a personal perspective depending on which way the viewer is facing, such as left, right, front or back; while other information relates to universal reference points like north, south, vertical and horizontal.

4. **Temporal perception**
   Understanding time, sequence and order.

5. **Representation**
   Human beings have developed innumerable ways of representing reality and ideas. These may be verbal, pictorial, graphic or symbolic, to name a few. Representation can be simple like the word 'blue'

representing the colour blue, or highly complex like mathematical symbols for a combination of abstract ideas. Students' performance will become limited at the point where they lose track of what representations and symbols mean.

6. **Comparison**
Understanding how things are equivalent, similar or different. Comparison is achieved by focusing on specific criteria in both a focus entity A, and a target entity B. It can be simple when one object is compared with another object; but it becomes highly complex when one system of interrelated elements is compared to another. For example, comparing the circulatory system of reptiles versus mammals. Comparison is the basis for categorisation because it reveals how things belong, or do not belong, in a group. When comparing, equivalence, similarity and difference can simply be noted. It is important to remember that depending on the feature that is the focus, a single entity can belong to more than one category. A red circle can belong to a colour category and shape category. This is the basis of Venn diagrams. At a higher level of thinking, comparison is the basis for decision-making and evaluation. A further fundamental aspect of comparison is to keep track of what remains the same and what has changed or transformed. For example, if six oranges have been cut in quarters, there are 24 pieces, but the fact remains that all the parts originate from six oranges. This is the conservation of constancy – tracking what is the same.

7. **Visualisation**
Mentally representing things in the mind. This may be a single visualisation or a complex manipulation of information. Visualisation can relate to the present, past and future.

8. **Identifying relationships**
Internal relationships exist between a whole and its parts. A person can move, because he or she has feet and legs. External

relationships exist between a whole and another whole. A torch, a lamp, a taillight and a chandelier are related because they all project light. Some relationships are determined with reference to a specific criterion internally or externally. One box is bigger, has greater volume, is sturdier than another. Relationships might be contextual. A nurse, hospital, ambulance and emergency care are related. Some relationships are causal: x happened because of y. I checked my Facebook and burnt the toast ... again.

9. **Problem-solving**
Problem solving has a process. Perceive a problem, assess it and develop a plan to solve it. Gather full and complete information, discard irrelevant information, combine more than one source of information, plan the sequence of steps, enact the steps, solve the problem.

10. **Providing logical evidence**
Using what is known, often from several different sources, to explain occurrences. It is related to inferential thinking whereby conclusions are drawn based on evidence.

11. **Hypothetical thinking**
Hypothetical thinking is 'if ... then' thinking. It is using available information to project what might happen, or to visualise alternatives. It is related to the scientific method but can be used in all areas of life.

12. **Imagination**
Imagination can occur at many levels. It can be a simple image, or it can lead to infinite possibilities. It is the fuel of creativity. Sir Ken Robinson considered the two in this way: 'Imagination allows us to think of things that aren't real or around us at any given time, creativity allows us to do something meaningful with our imaginations' (Robinson & Aronica 2010).

5 Senses Words

sight	blind, blurry, clear, dark, glance, glimpse, keen, light, observe, outlook, panorama, peripheral vision, range of vision, scenery, see, sight, spy, stare, survey, unclear, visibility, vista, witness
sound	alliteration, animal sounds, bang and crash sounds, distant, drone, echo, high, insect sounds, knock, loud, low, mechanical sounds, movement sounds, musical pitch, natural sounds, onomatopoeia, rattles, sibilance, sirens, signals, soft, volume, weather sounds
taste	acidic, bitter, chewy, creamy, crisp, crumbly, crunchy, dense, dry, el dente, fluffy, fresh, gelatinous, granular, gritty, herby, hot, light, liquid lumpy, oily, powdery, runny, saccharine, salty, savoury, smooth, soggy, solid, sour, spicy, stale, stodgy, sweet, tart

smell	aromatic, cloying, damp, fetid, floral, foul, fragrant, fresh, fumes, herby, malodorous, musty, perfumed, pleasant, pungent, smoky, spicy, sweet
touch	ache, agony, bruised, bumpy, cold, constricted, corrugated, crackly, cramp, crisp, dry, firm, fluffy, furry, fuzzy, gritty, grooved, hard, hot, icy, itchy, loose, lumpy, massage, moist, mushy, numb, oily, painful, pat, pinch, pins and needle, plump, prickly, pummel, ridged, rough, rubbery, satiny, scaly, scratchy, silky, slap, slippery, smack, smooth, soft, sore, spongy, stroke, swollen, tickly, tight, velvety, warm, waxy, woolly, wrinkly

Weather Words

breezy, bright, cloudy, cold, cool, fog, hail, humid, mild, mist, overcast, rain, sleet, snow, storm, sunny, thunder and lightning, warm, windy

10 Modalities for Learning

1. **Concrete:** using or manipulating objects in the real world.

2. **Verbal:** related to the use of language for accessing, assessing, processing or expressing learning. There are two main aspects to the verbal modality: oral and written.

3. **Symbolic:** related to any symbols either recognised or developed to represent something else. Examples are road signs, letters, numbers, the table of elements. Students can create their own symbols to represent information or understand the symbols in their daily life and curriculum.

4. **Pictorial:** relates to images that are representative of reality, such as life-like drawings or photographic materials. Pictorial is differentiated from graphic below because pictures are less abstract and more accessible than graphic formats. Graphic formats may have some symbolic elements that have to be learned.

5. **Figural:** relates to anything to do with form or shape.

6. **Graphic:** relates to drawings that may or may not include easily recognisable representations of information. Examples are line drawings and graphic organisers. The drawings are more abstract than pictures and may include some elements of what it is representing. Or it relates to a representative way to encapsulate complex information in an easily absorbed format, for example, graphs, diagrams, models.

7. **Digital:** refers to any use of digital devices and may include many other modalities. Digital technology enables students to combine many modalities quickly and easily and it requires a particular kind of technological skill and know-how.

8. **Kinaesthetic:** refers to capturing information in movement. This can be single movements and sensation captured through the senses or a complex sequence of movements. Movement and sensation are harnessed as a vehicle for complex communication (embodied cognition).

9. **Representational/metaphorical:** refers to the ability to develop an idea or concept that represents some aspect of an object, relationship or abstract concept. It usually makes it easier for the learner to comprehend the complexity of something else through something that is known or understood.

10. **Imaginary:** relates to the ability of the mind to explore new ideas or knowledge. This can be a fairly simple or an extremely complex mental construct for learning and problem-solving.

Play Ideas and Equipment

Social, Emotional and Cultural Concepts and Skills

Home Corner	Imaginary Play Themes	Outdoor Play
Furniture:	castle	A-frames
bed	cultural	balancing beams
bookcase	cultural celebrations	baskets
chairs	fairy tale	brooms
cot	fire station	buckets
cupboard	hair salon	climbing rocks
divider	home/kitchen	cooking utensils
sink	medical	digger trucks
stove	office	fabric
table	police	fixed climbing, swinging, flying fox, etc.
	school	
Props:	shop	
bed clothes	superheroes	large building blocks
dolls	transport	musical chimes
dress-up items		platforms
empty grocery containers		PVC piping
play money		rakes
pots and pans		sandpit
scale		scrapers
tea set		see saw
wooden people		spades
		watering cans
		woodwork equipment

Sports and Activities	Recycled and Decorative Materials	Construction and Table-Top Toys
	bottles	
balls	cardboard boxes	
bean bags	cardboard cylinders	blocks
big blocks	dowel sticks	DUPLO®
cycles	jars	games
hockey	lengths of fabric	gears
hoola hoops	lengths of timber	LASY
lengths of rope	natural materials	LEGO®
natural materials	plastic containers	matching and sorting
parachute	rubber	Meccano®
quoits	timber offcuts	puzzles
skipping ropes	various	sequencing
skittles	manufacturing	stickle bricks
soccer	offcuts	tessellation
walking stilts	wishing stones	What's in a Square

Social, Emotional and Cultural Concepts and Skills

Self-care and home skills
Dressing, bedtime, bath time, mealtime, pet care, travel and commuting, play, cooking and baking, setting the table, building and construction, setting up and packing away.

Gross and fine motor skills
Pick up food and objects, use cutlery, use crockery, lift body, roll, sit, crawl, bounce, balance, walk, run, hop, skip, jump, roll, slide, climb, swing, hang, alternate movements fluidly, pinch, clasp, lift, cut, paste, carry objects, arrange materials, hold and use painting, drawing and writing implements, roll (e.g. plasticine and clay), stack objects and balance objects.

Social and cultural concepts
Identity, self, other, people, humanity, relationship, emotion, friendship, family, culture, society, religion, love, respect and inclusion.

Social interactions
Greet others, make eye contact (if culturally appropriate), engage in conversation, take turns, see things from another's point of view, help others, accept help from others, be cooperative, be collaborative, be aware of what is happening in the environment, take care of another, self-regulate behaviour, self-regulate emotions, move beyond the need for instant gratification, engage in rites of passage, share in cultural events, understand roles and rituals in different cultures, religions and ethnic groups.

Emotional intelligence (EQ)
Understand emotions, name emotions, understand others' emotions, name others' emotions, develop self-talk strategies to withstand negative emotions, develop a routine/strategy for dealing with conflict, be empathetic, be sympathetic, understand boundaries, respect boundaries, understand the consequences of behaviours, deal with the consequences of behaviours, learn to separate the person from the behaviour, understand that no emotional state is permanent, predict emotional impact, and accept that emotions are part of life.

Curriculum Areas to Explore

Arts and crafts:

- Drama
- Puppetry
- Mark making
- Interpret images and artworks
- Design and execute 2D and 3D products
- Understand space and spatial relationships
- Understand time and temporal relationships
- Understand materials and how they may be used
- Organise marks and/or ideas on page or canvas
- Interpret and investigate gesture and body language
- Learn about motion, posture and the interpretative dance.

Science and nature:

- Electricity
- Magnetism
- Properties of air
- Carry out experiments
- Energy and combustion
- Growth and development
- Life cycles of animals and plants
- Observe and record information
- Develop and test hypotheses
- Melting, freezing and evaporation of water
- Food processes during baking and cooking
- Physical properties of matter, e.g. glue dries hard
- Biological processes: breathing, nutrition, digestion
- Modes of communication: digital, wireless, internet
- The senses: processes of sight, hearing, touch, taste, smell
- The brain: thinking, imagining, creating, connecting, learning, etc.

Mathematics:

- Counting
- Estimate
- Measure
- Graph
- Build patterns
- Add and subtract
- Divide and multiply
- Number knowledge
- Collect and sort materials
- Make groups and sets
- Understand terminology
- Understand symbols
- Explain relationships
- Geometric shapes and attendant knowledge
- Understand grouping symbols for equations
- Represent the ideas in numerical, spatial, concrete and other ways
- Apply/transfer mathematical procedures as listed above.

Verbal literacy (this includes oral speech and written language):

- Listen to sounds
- Identify sounds
- Talk in single words
- Combine words
- Use sentences
- Identify words and match them with real world equivalents
- Identify words with what is known but is not immediately present
- Identify words with what is neither known nor immediately present using imagination
- Listen to stories
- Monitor the sequence and plot

- Understand stories
- Tell stories
- Remember and relate experiences
- Understand similarities and differences
- Identify causal relationships
- Predict events and routines
- Visualise
- Follow conversations
- Recognise that a book uses language of image and word
- Know that images and words have meaning
- Recognise written words
- Read words and sounds
- Identify images
- Understand images
- Read sounds
- Read words
- Read sentences
- Read full texts
- Read stories
- Identify characters
- Identify relationships between characters
- Follow the plot
- Follow the argument of structure of a text
- Distinguish what is more and less important
- Understand the chronological aspects of the narrative
- Understand analogies
- Understand what is implicit in the text
- Understand different formats of text
- Understand how the text is organised

Thank you for taking the time to read this book.

For more information or to get in touch, visit my website:

https://www.kriegler-education.com

References

ACMI 2020, *Making Wonderland Documentary*. Retrieved from YouTube October 9 2020, https://www.youtube.com/watch?v=rnIquw8qYgO&ab_channel=ACMI%28AustralianCentrefortheMovingImage%29

Atherton, F & Nutbrown, C 2013, *Understanding Schemas and Young Children - Birth to Three*, SAGE, London.

Anderson, L. Kratwohl, D, Airasian, P, Mayer, R, Pintrich, P, Wittrock, M (Eds.) 2001, *A taxonomy for learning, teaching and assessing*, Longman, New York.

Baratta-Lorton, M 1994, *Mathematics Their Way: An Activity-Centered Mathematics Program for Early Childhood Education,* Pearson.

Bartlett, B 2003, 'Valuing the situation: a referential outcome for top-level structures', *Reimagining Practice: Researching Change*, vol. 1, pp. 16–37.

Ben-Hur, M 2006, *Concept-rich Mathematics Instruction*, Association for Supervision and Curriculum Development, USA.

Biggs, J 2016, *Academic, SOLO Taxonomy*. Retrieved March 9, 2016, from John Biggs, writer, traveller, academic: http://www.johnbiggs.com.au/

Bodrova, E & Leong, DJ 1996, *Tools of the Mind - the Vygotskian Approch to Early Childhood Education*, Prentice-Hall Inc, New Jersey.

Bruner, J 1973, 'Going beyond the information given', In Anglin, J, *Beyond the information given* (pp. 218–238), Norton, New York.

Buzan, T 2010, *Use Your Head - how to unleash the power of your mind*, Pearson Education, Harlow, UK.

Buzan, T & Buzan, B 1993, *The Mind Map Book*, Butler and Tanner, London.

Cagliari, P, Castagnetti, M. Giudici, C, Rinaldi, C, Vecchi, V, & Moss, P 2016, *Loris Malaguzzi and the Schools of Reggio Emilia: A selection of his writings and speeches, 1945-1993*, Routledge, New York.

Castagnetti, M, & Vecchi, V (Eds.) 1997, *Shoe and Meter (Scapra e Metro)*. Reggio Emilia: Reggio Children.

Costa, A 2008, *Learning and Leading with Habits of Mind*, Association for Supervision and Curriculum Development, USA.

Covey, S 2013, *The 7 Habits of Highly Effective People (Electronic Edition)*. Rosetta Books LLC.

Darling-Hammond, L, Barron, B, Pearson, DP, Schoenfeld, AH, Stage, EK, Zimmerman, TD, Chen, M 2008, *Powerful Learning - what we understand about teaching for understanding*, Jossey-Bass, San Francisco.

De Bono, E 1993, *Serious Creativity – Using the Power of Lateral Thinking to Create New Ideas*, Harper Collins, Glasgow.

De Bono, E 1998, *Lateral thinking & the use of lateral thinking*, Penguin Books, Australia.

Doenmez, S 2020, *The Threshold Concept Framework Can Lead to Transformative Learning*. Retrieved from NAIS (National Association of Independent Schools) October 5 2020, https://www.nais.org/magazine/independent-school/summer-2018/threshold-concept-framework/

Donaldson, M 1984, *Children's Minds*, Fontana, London.

Dweck, C 2006, *Mindset: The New Psychology of Success*, Random House, New York.

Eather, J 2020, *A Maths Dictionary for Kids*. Retrieved from A Maths Dictionary for Kids October 7 2020, http://www.amathsdictionaryforkids.com/

Edwards, C, Gandini, L, & Foreman, EG (Eds.) 1998, *The Hundred Languages of Children: The Reggio Emilia Approach advanced perspectives*, Ablex Publishing Corporation, Greenwich.

Education.com. 2020, *Bouncing Ball Physics: What is Elasticity*. Retrieved from Education.com November 21 2020, https://www.education.com/science-fair/article/ball-bounce-higher-dropped-greater-height/

Ellis, K, Denton, D & Bond, J 2013, 'An analysis of research on metacognitive teaching strategies', *Procedia Social and Behavioural Sciences*, pp. 4015-4024.

Epstein, D 2019, *Range,* Pan Macmillan, London.

Falikman, MV 2014, 'Cognition and its master: new challenges for cognitive science', In Yasnitsky, A, Van der Veer, R & Ferrari, M (Eds.), *The Cambridge Handbook of Cutlrual-Historical Psychology*, Cambridge University Press, UK.

Feuerstein Institute, 2020, *International Centre for Enhanced Learning Potential (ICELP)*, Retrieved September 17 2020 from https://www.icelp.info/

Feuerstein, R, Feuerstein, R & Falik, L 2009, *The Feuerstein Instrumental Enrichment Basic Program,* The Feuerstein Institute, Jerusalem.

Feuerstein, R, Rand, Y, Hoffman, M, & Miller, R 1980, *Instrumental Enrichment: An Intervention Program for Cognitive Modifiability*, Scott, Foresman & Co, Glenview, Illinois.

Gardner, H 1993, *Frames of Mind – The theory of multiple intelligences,* Fontana Press, London.

Gardner, H 2000, *The Disciplined Mind,* Penguin, Hammondsworth, UK.

Gentner, D 2005, 'The Development of Relational Category Knowledge', In Geschkoff, L & Rakison, DH *Building Object Categories in Developmental Time* (pp. 245–275), Erlbaum, New Jersey.

Goldsworthy, A 1989, *A collaboration with nature*, Green Apple Books, Abrams.

Goleman, D 1995, *Emotional Intelligence*, Bantam, New York.

Guskey, TR 2001, *Benjamin S. Bloom's Contributions to Curriculum, Instruction and School Learning*, University of Kentucky.

Hansen, A 2013, BCS curriculum in kindergarten and school 2009, https://researchgate.net/publication/258316586

Hill, R 2016, *Kant's Schematism and Time Determinations*, Retrieved from Expordium e-journal: https://exordiumuq.org/2016/07/19/kants-schematism-and-time-determinations-by-rosie-hill/

Horvath, JC 2019), *Stop talking and start influencing*, Exisle Publishing, Chatswood.

IBO 2020, *Primary Years Program*. Retrieved from International Baccalaureate Organisation 14 September 2020, https://www.ibo.org/programmes/primary-years-programme/

Kilpatrick, J, Swafford, J & Bradford, E 2001, *Adding it up: Helping children learn mathematics,* National Academy Press, Washington D.C.

Kinard, JT & Kozulin, A 2008, *Rigorous Mathematical Thinking,* Cambridge University Press, UK.

McLeod, S 2019, *What is the zone of proximal development?* Retrieved from Simply Psychology 5 December 2020, https://www.simplypsychology.org/Zone-of-Proximal-Development.html

Meadows, S 1993, *The Child as Thinker – the Development and Acquisition for Cognition in Childhood* (First Edition ed.), Routledge, Guildford, UK.

Montessori, M 1965, *Dr Montessori's own notebook,* Schocken Books, New York.

Piaget, J & Cook, MT 1952, *The Origins of Intelligence in Children,* International University Press, New York.

Project Zero; Reggio Children 2001, *Making Learning Visible – Children as Indicidual and Group Learners,* (C. Giudici, & M. Krechevsky, Eds.) Reggio Children, Reggio Emilia, Italy.

Rieber, RW & Carton, AS (Eds.) 1987, 'Thinking and Speech', In *The collected works of L.S. Vygotsky. Vol 1: Problems for general psychology,* Plenum Press Development, New York.

Rinaldi, C 2001, 'The Pedagogy of Listening', *Innovations in early education: the international reggio exchange,* Vol 8, no.4.

Robinson, K & Aronica, L 2010, *The Element: How finding your passion changes everything,* Penguin, London.

Ronilo, A 2018, 'Effectiveness of metacognitive instruction on students' science learning achievement: A meta-analysis, *SSRN.*

Schonkoff, JP, Phillips, DA & (Eds.) 2000, *From Neurons to Neighbourhoods – The science of early childhood development,* The National Academy of Sciences, Washington D.C.

Sherrington, CS 1955, *Man on his nature,* Penguin Books, Harmonsworth.

Singer, DG, Golinkoff, RM & Hirsh-Pasek, K 2006, *Play=Learning: How Play Motivates and Enhances Children's Cognitive and Social-Emotional Growth,* Oxford Univeristy Press, New York.

Skemp, RR, 1986, *The psychology of learning mathematics,* Plenum, Middlesex.

Stuart, JE 1911, *The Education of Catholic Girls,* The Gutenberg Project.

Suskind, D 2015, *Thrty Million Words – Building a Child's Brain*, Dutton, New York.

Vygotsky, L 1978, *Mind in Society: The development of higher psychological processes*, Harvard University Press, Cambridge.

Vygotsky, L 1986, *Thought and language (Kozulin, A translated and Ed.)*, MIT Press, Cambridge.

Walker, K & Bass, S 2015, *Early Childhood Play Matters,* ACER Press, Melbourne.

Watanabe-Crockett, L 2018, *Future-focused learning,* Solution Tree, US.

WEHImovies 2020, *Organelles of a Human Cell*, Retrieved from YouTube 28 September 2020, https://www.youtube.com/watch?v=2YCgro6BV8U&ab_channel=WEHImovies

Whitely, G (Director) 2015, *Most Likely to Succeed* [Motion Picture].

Wikipedia 2020, *Holography*, Retrieved from Wikipedia 29 September 2020, https://en.wikipedia.org/wiki/Holography

Yasnitsky, A, Van Der Veer, R, Ferrari, M & (Eds.) 2014, *The Cambridge Handbook of Cultural-Historical Psychology*, Cambridge University Press, Cambridge.

Zhu, P 2016, *Digital Agility: The rocky road from doing agile to being agile,* https://www.amazon.com.au/Digital-Agility-Rocky-Doing-Master-ebook/dp/B01GSE77XE

SPEAKER BIOGRAPHY
LILI-ANN KRIEGLER

'I BELIEVE IN THE TRANSFORMATIVE POWER OF EDUCATION'

EDU-CHAMELEON
Leverage 7 Dynamic Learning Zones to Enhance Young Children's Concept-Based Understanding

Lili-Ann is an education consultant and author with experience at all levels of education.

Based on her M.Ed studies and 30 years' experience in the field, she provides consultancy in curriculum design, concept-based teaching, school transition for enhanced thinking and pedagogical leadership. She is a senior trainer for the Feuerstein Institute, the International Centre for Enhanced Cognitive Potential.

Lili-Ann is an engaging speaker. In her presentations, whether to small workshop groups or auditoriums, her knowledge is peppered with stories and practical examples. She is able to tailor presentations to the specific needs of schools and groups of educators. She also does one on one mentoring sessions for educators.

PRESENTATIONS

Be an Edu-Chameleon and use 7 learning zones to boost children's conceptual understanding

- Explore 7 dynamic teaching zones on the agility wheel
- Use your flexible knowledge to enhance curriculum planning
- Become an expert assessor of children's concept learning
- Breakout your own aspirations and creativity

Supercharge children's learning with just 6 organising concepts

- Unpack 6 foundational learning concepts
- Learn the 5 step process to teach them
- Use a simple, but effective assessment tool to keep track of children's concept-based understanding

Implement the 8 essential actions of high achieveing educational leadeers

- Explore the 8 essential actions that will boost your leadership for teams
- Use five steps to enhance planning and assessment across the board
- Apply the steps to transform educator practice and enhance student outcomes

Email: lili-ann@kriegler-education.com; or visit www.kriegler-education.com to make a booking.
Mobile: +61-438489032

About the Author

Lili-Ann was born in Johannesburg, South Africa, and lived with her parents Bob and Bee Erasmus, and siblings Helene´ and Martin. Her father worked on the gold mines so the family relocated several times. As a child she loved spending time with her grandparents and on one of her visits, they went to a local fair. There were highland dancers performing and she loved it so much she immediately hopped up on stage with them! Consequently, she had her first ballet lesson at age four and she also loved piano lessons. Enid Blyton was her favourite author and she constantly entertained her siblings with her own made up stories. When the family lived in Virginia, a country mining town, the children roamed freely in the neighbourhood. After school she would load her siblings onto a wooden wagon made by her grandpa and pull them into town to borrow books from the library. She has always loved going to the theatre and was mesmerised by puppet shows her primary teachers put on at school. All of these early influences continue to resonate in her life today.

Lili-Ann boarded at Eunice High School in Bloemfontein for her last two years of secondary school. After that she resided on campus at the University of the Witwatersrand to complete an education degree. During that time, she met Pierre, her husband, and they have made a wonderful life together with their son, Sean, and daughter, Candice. The family has travelled widely in Europe and America and skiing is their favourite holiday activity. Lili-Ann loves being active and what many don't know about her is that she earned Springbok national colours in South Africa for race walking!

The most significant and best decision the family made was to move to Australia in 1998.

Lili-Ann is passionate about education and completed a variety of courses culminating in a master's degree in education and leadership. Her life journey also included wonderful side-steps into fashion design, floristry and puppetry.

During her career she has taught at all levels. In Melbourne, she had a sojourn at Bialik College and was Director of Early Learning at Fintona Girls' School for a decade. Her current role is as an education consultant at Independent Schools Victoria (ISV). Her time at ISV has afforded her many opportunities including becoming a trainer in Feuerstein Instrumental Enrichment, which focuses on human cognition.

Apart from education, Lili-Ann is a keen golfer (some would say it is an addiction!). Her favourite place to play is at the home of golf, St. Andrews in Scotland.

She enjoys Rotary and has been club president. One of most interesting Rotary endeavours was creating 'The Waggle Dance' to raise awareness about the global importance of bees and pollinators for food security. Many will know that bees do a waggle dance to communicate to their hive where to find pollen and nectar. Bees are vital for the planet and she and Pierre have a hive in their garden.

She loves spending time with friends and family, especially visiting her siblings in the UK and Spain.

Lili-Ann plans to continue working as an education consultant.

To get in touch with Lili-Ann, visit her website: https://www.kriegler-education.com

Acknowledgements

Where do you start to acknowledge everyone who makes your work and your challenge a reality? There are so many people who have influenced my thinking, my career and my aspirations. I start by thanking my husband for his constant support, incisive comments, forward propulsion and patience. Pierre you are without a doubt, the 'wind beneath my wings'. I acknowledge my miraculous and amazing adult children, Sean and Candice. I thank you for your enthusiastic interest in all my endeavours. (Even the crazy ones!)

I am grateful to my late parents, Bob and Bee, for instilling a lifelong belief in the power of education and for their encouragement and support. Likewise, to my siblings, Helene and Martin, who have achieved great things in their lives based on the same foundations.

I thank all the colleagues I have worked with since I started my career in South Africa and in my time working in this enviable country, Australia. I have learned with you and from you every day as we enacted our roles shoulder to shoulder.

I would like to make a special mention of two valued mentors, Jan Millikan OAM and Genia Janover. Your contribution to me personally and to education in general cannot be quantified.

Professional learning is mandated for educators, and I have participated in so many important programs throughout my career. But two of these journeys need to be highlighted. The knowledge I have gained from my encounters with the Reggio Emilia philosophy and the education absorbed from the Feuerstein Institute have been game changers for me.

My sojourn as an education consultant at Independent Schools Victoria has opened vistas and I am grateful to CE, Michelle Green, for all the opportunities afforded me in this role.

To my dear colleague and friend, Helen Schiele, your partnership in our past endeavours, has made this book both possible and a reality.

To the team at Ultimate 48 Hour Author, your professionalism, knowledge, support and wisdom has made this journey infinitely more achievable and I thank you all.

To all my friends and family spread far and wide, your interest and support is greatly appreciated.

Offers

Please visit my website where you can use the access code 'chameleonzone' to:

- Download PDF version of the diagrams
- Download the Edu-Chameleon lists in Part D of this book in an A3 format
- Book a complimentary 30-minute online introductory Q&A session
- Access a complimentary 40-minute recorded introduction to concept-based teaching
- Book a consultancy regarding any of the topics on my speaker biography, or request a customised professional learning encounter

Visit: https://www.kriegler-education.com

Email: liliannk@icloud.com

Please write to me to share your concept-based teaching successes. I love hearing from educators!

'I believe in the transformational power of education.'

Best wishes

Lili-Ann Kriegler

Reflections

www.ingramcontent.com/pod-product-compliance
Lightning Source LLC
Chambersburg PA
CBHW020033120526
44588CB00030B/153